STOP TELLING
START ASKING

HOW TO DEVELOP THE PEOPLE AROUND YOU
BY **ASKING** THE RIGHT QUESTIONS

D1059636

STOP TELLING START ASKING

HOW TO DEVELOP THE PEOPLE AROUND YOU BY **ASKING** THE RIGHT QUESTIONS

Maureen Blanchfield Kolb

Stop Telling. Start Asking: How to Develop the People Around You by Asking the Right Questions by Maureen Blanchfield Kolb
© 2011 by Maureen Blanchfield Kolb

Editor: Anne Bingham
Cover design: Doug Fellows and Kate Hawley
Cover image: iStockphoto
Interior design: Sue Knopf, Graffolio
Production consultant: Susan Pittelman

Published 2011
Printed in the United States of America

15 14 13 12 11   1 2 3 4 5

ISBN-13: 978-0-9835780-0-0
Library of Congress Control Number: 2011927991

Publisher's Cataloging-in-Publication
(*Provided by Quality Books, Inc.*)

Kolb, Maureen Blanchfield.
    Stop telling, start asking : how to develop the people around you by asking the right questions / Maureen Blanchfield Kolb. — 1st ed.
    p. cm.
    LCCN 2011927991
    ISBN-13: 978-0-9835780-0-0
    ISBN-10: 0-9835780-0-1
    1. Leadership. 2. Employees—Training of.
I. Title.
    HD57.7.K56 2011   658.4'092
                    QBI11-600101

Published by Cr8ive Energies Press
8008 North Poplar Drive
Fox Point, WI 53217
(414) 350-9034
maureen@Cr8iveEnergies.com
www.Cr8iveEnergies.com

To Keith, of course.

Contents

Introduction

More than ten years ago, one of the largest accounting firms
in the world hired me to coach its senior managers,
people who were one step away from partner.
My first question to each of the almost-partners was,
"Why do you want to be a partner?"
Each person gave me the same startled answer:
"No one has ever asked me that before."

Over the course of years, I have become recognized as a coach to senior executives for my ability to take common sense one step further by asking the right questions. The positive energy this creates helps them

- Find the energy to move forward when all they want to do is run and hide.

- Ask the difficult question no one else wants to ask, in a way that engages others in the room instead of alienating them.

- Lead by asking questions rather than by mandating, in order to develop future leaders who will approach issues the same way.

- Pause when they are dying to parachute into the middle of a sticky situation and solve things.

It has been my privilege—and challenge—to work as an executive coach to some of America's finest corporate leaders. Each has his or her own management style and way of looking at the world, but for all that, the question I am asked most often in the initial interview is, "If you were my coach and you could give me just one piece of advice, what would it be?"

My response is always the same: *Develop the people around you.*

·   ·   ·

If you died tomorrow, who would take your place at work? Do you have a solid team ready to keep the business running? If you don't, you haven't been a successful leader because you haven't developed your people.

And the best way to develop them is by asking questions.

The leaders for whom everyone wants to work are the ones who spend their time developing others, not by telling them what to do, but by asking questions that force the people around them to think, and rethink, their approaches. They ask how you might accomplish something, rather than telling you how to do it.

Let me give you a simple example.

My husband and I own a thirty-three-foot boat that we keep in dry stack. When we want to use our boat, we call the marina and they put it in the water for us. Juan, the forklift driver, picks up the boat from the garage and carefully places it in the lake. Although I am in awe of this process, I get a little sick to my stomach as I watch our boat sway twenty feet in the air on its way from the garage to the lake.

One day I asked Juan, "How did you learn to drive that thing?"

"Tim taught me. At first he was the only one who knew how to drive the lift. One day he realized that if a truck hit him, a lot of people would not be able to enjoy their boats. It took me a while to get it right. I actually dropped a small boat the first time, and I poked holes in a few others. But Tim made me keep trying, always asking me what gear I was using, what level made sense, did I think the prongs were low enough in the water.

"Eventually I got it," he went on. "Now he wants me to teach the other guys."

. . .

This is not a self-help book or a book about how to take care of your staff. It is a how-to-help-others book that will show you how to care for your leadership team in such a way that you help them grow.

It won't always be easy. Sometimes what you have to do to help another person grow is not what that person wants. Genuine growth always involves a certain amount of pain—or at least, a letting go—and senior executives can be as resistant to change as the most territorial zone manager. This is why I start every coaching relationship with the caveat: "This will not always be fun, and you will not always like me."

But I can guarantee that if you can change your approach from telling people what to do to asking them what they would do, you will see dramatic results in a relatively short time.

In this book I share several executive coaching experiences. In some cases the leader and I were wildly successful. In other cases we failed, and I'm up front about what went wrong. Sometimes I was the one who missed an important clue to the organizational dynamic, sometimes the client was just not interested in changing his or her approach. Because confidentiality is a given, I've thoroughly disguised the identities of the individuals and corporations involved. At times, I have mixed a few coaching experiences together, some of the stories are a more-than-one-client experience, but I assure you, the situations are genuine. They really happened, and if you have been in a leadership role for more than a few months, you probably will recognize something close to a situation at your own workplace.

1

Why We Don't Ask Questions

If your ability to develop others truly lies in your ability to ask good questions, then why don't you do it more often? There are several reasons.

First, childhood experiences often discourage children from asking questions.

When you were three years old and your parents took you to visit your grandparents, what were you encouraged to do? Ask Grandma questions?

Probably not. Your job was to show Grandma what you'd learned.

"Sing that new song you learned at camp, Trish!"

"Heather, you say the alphabet for Grandma."

"How does the turkey go, Brad?"

Think about the quiet children you know, the ones who sit back and observe rather than jumping into the center of attention. Do other parents brag that Tanya is a really good observer, or that Zack is a great listener?

Not in the real world. Instead, teachers report that "Tanya is a shy child. She keeps to herself," and that Zachary "needs to work on his social skills." The child who gets all the positive reinforcement is the one who's delighted to gobble-gobble on cue no matter how unfamiliar the situation.

Something else that works against kids learning that it's okay to ask questions is parental fatigue. Most children are naturally inquisitive, and they tend to overdo it at certain stages in their development. Parents understandably slip up from time to time, especially at the end of a long day, and find themselves exclaiming something along the lines of, "Drew, if you ask one more question I am going to Lose. My. Mind."

So you probably were not rewarded for asking questions during your early childhood years except in the artificial sense of "participating in class," and even that depends more on taking part in a discussion than asking questions.

Fast-forward to high school, which in all but the best cases requires students to master a subject sufficiently to pass whatever competency test is being required that particular year. What would happen if a teacher in an American History class decided to develop his or her students' levels of intellectual curiosity rather than the students' abilities in R&R—Read and Regurgitate—and then based students' grades on what happened when they were assigned a portion of the Constitution and told to design five questions that would demonstrate their understanding of that portion of the Constitution?

Odds are there would be a conversation or two between parents and the principal about the testing practices of this teacher.

So the second reason that asking questions pushes against your comfort level is that you've been trained to have the answer, not the question. Most of you spent sixteen-plus years in school being judged on your ability to answer questions correctly. Then you headed out into the rest of your life and what happened? You kept right on answering questions, not asking them, because all your training was in providing answers.

The third reason is that you've been taught that questions that mean anything are impolite. That goes back to being shushed when you ask why Grandma has hair on her upper lip and Grandpa doesn't have any on the top of his head, right on up to asking people how much money they make or how much they paid for their house.

That was then, and that was learning the basics of etiquette and tact.

This is now, and this is business. There is a big difference between asking questions about things that are none of your business and asking questions to develop your leadership team. It's the difference between asking "What makes you think you look good in green?" and "What do you think are the reasons your division didn't make your sales goal this year?"

Finally, asking questions goes against the "tell, not sell" model that characterizes American business. When you want someone to better understand a process, or an opinion, or an opportunity, you generally tell them *why* the process is better, or *why* this opinion is the right one, or *why* they need to consider an opportunity.

Generally, an if-then statement is involved.

For instance, here's the owner of a small printing company speaking to her press foreman:

"If you get this order out the door by five o'clock this afternoon, then your team can go home."

"If you don't get this order out the door by five o'clock this afternoon, then your team will have to stay late to finish it."

Whichever way she phrases it, she has not engaged the other party; she's told them what will happen…and created a lose-lose situation for both parties.

How could you handle the situation to engage the other party?

Ask a question.

Here's the same printing company owner, speaking to the same press foreman, only this time she asks:

"What will happen if this order isn't out by five o'clock?"

"I suppose we'll get it out first thing in the morning," the foreman replies.

"Do you know if this customer needs the order by tomorrow morning, or are they flexible?"

"I don't know. Let me check with sales."

"Great. Are you comfortable making a decision based on what sales tells you?"

"Yes."

"Is there anything I can do to help you get this done?"

"I'll let you know."

What's just happened here? The owner doesn't have to be the bad guy!

She doesn't have to bring down the hammer to get the job done or tell the foreman he has to mandate overtime. Instead, she engages him in the decision-making process. There's no whining or gnashing of teeth. She puts the dilemma in the foreman's hands and authorizes him to resolve it.

And that's what it's all about: putting the dilemma in the minds of others and giving them the authority to resolve it. When you give your employees the opportunity to come up with a solution on their own, they almost always come up with a good one.

But instead, most leaders tell them what needs to be done. It's easier and seems quicker in the short term, but as a business executive, your job is to focus on the long-term interests of the company, so it's time to... *Stop Telling and Start Asking.*

Have you ever been to an Apple store to have your computer fixed? These are some of the best-trained technicians in the world. Watch what they do! The technician tells you very little during the first five minutes. Instead, he or she asks questions: *What were you doing when the problem started? Have you had the problem before? What programs were open? Did lightning strike anywhere in the neighborhood before the screen started to melt?*

The tech is narrowing down the possibilities to try to determine what went wrong. (Okay, the tech also is running a diagnostic and some of the questions just *might* be a way to kill time until the diagnostic kicks out its results, but the point is, the tech is asking for your input.)

Like many executives, you probably believe it's your job to have all the answers. Maybe you do have all the answers! But you cannot develop your people if you *tell* them what to do. You must ask them.

Every one of you has had a moment when you've asked a question and the other person looks at you, cocks his or her head and says, "That's a really good question." To me, that's the biggest compliment someone can give.

In order to develop other people, you need to ask them more of those "really good" questions—questions that make them think about the future, questions that force them to remember the past, questions that help them learn more about themselves and how they are in the world. Questions that make them think.

So get over what you learned as a kid. Get ready to learn how to ask questions that will develop your people more than anything else you do or have ever done for them. Asking the right questions is far more important than giving someone the right answers. You are teaching them to fish, not just giving them a fish. I believe the key to leading and developing others is by asking rather than telling. Let's get to work!

THE CHALLENGE
Start Listening for Questions

For the next week, notice people who ask a lot of questions in both your professional and personal lives. People who have this skill tend to use it often. If you pay attention, you can learn from them. Make note of who the questioners are, then log what kinds of questions they ask, how they ask them, how valuable their questions are, whether they wait for answers.

- *What kinds of questions do they ask?* Do they ask open-ended questions and wait for the answers, such as "What month makes the most sense for our global meeting?"

Open-ended questions signal that the asker is willing to listen to all types of ideas and encourages brainstorming and creative thinking. Closed questions require only a Yes or No answer, and move people to resolution and results.

Both kinds of questions have their place. When I was recruiting actuaries for a client who wanted candidates with five years of experience, I couldn't get them to even consider a new opportunity. They were all very happy where they were. Finally I came up with the golden closed question: "Are you going to retire at the firm where you presently work?" They were only 27 years old. That question was the one that got their attention.

- *How do they ask questions?* Do they fire off a barrage of questions? Or do they ask one at a time so that people can respond thoughtfully to each one? People who fire off a barrage of questions are not listening for an answer. Rather, they are thinking out loud and have no interest in the answer.

- *How valuable are the questions?* Rhetorical questions have a place in the world, but irrelevant or hostile questions do not. Is the asker trying to make other people realize how much he knows, or rambling off-topic, or is his question truly to the point? Listen for those questions that make you say, "That is a really good question."

- *Does the questioner wait for an answer?* Some people abuse questions. They throw so many at you that you cannot begin to respond. Again, these people are not listening, nor are they interested in the answers to their questions. It is important to listen to how people use questions; it is equally important to note whether they get answers.

Awareness is 90 percent of the battle. As soon as you start being aware of others who are asking questions, you will become more aware of your own opportunities, and the rest will start to fall into place. Pay attention!

To help you become aware of questioners and their questioning techniques I suggest you use a small notebook or a pad of paper. Keep it with you at all times. When you hear someone asking questions write down their name, the questions they asked, whether they got an answer or not, and if the answer they got actually answered the question. If you do this, it won't take long for you to start naturally hearing interrogative statements. After writing them down for one month, you will begin to hear them naturally. This is the first step toward your journey of Stop Telling and Start Asking.

2

Give the Benefit of the Doubt

Duane works for a large consumer products company. He loves the company, the product, and his marketing team, which he built from the ground up in his six years with the firm. Things were going fine until Duane's boss made an organizational change that resulted in Duane reporting to someone else. At first, Duane wasn't worried. He knew his division was growing so fast that his original supervisor had been seriously overworked.

His new boss, Troy, is a 25-year veteran in the consumer products industry. It soon became apparent that Troy was a classic "product marketing guy" in the Procter and Gamble mode. The problem with this is that Duane is a classic "Madison Avenue guy," from the agency side. The two men could not have been more different in marketing skills or their approach to marketing.

Troy is a closed-door guy, Duane is an open-door guy.

Troy thinks Duane is too close to his team, "too buddy-buddy," as he phrased it in an email. Email is part of the problem. Duane thinks Troy acts like a hermit who sits in his office writing novel-length, and unnecessary, emails.

Duane calls me for help.

· · ·

The first question I ask Duane is, "What do you want your relationship with Troy to look like?"

"I want the guy to come out of his office and talk with me," he replies. "His door is always closed. When I knock and look into his window, he's always on the phone and he waves me away. His emails are four pages long, and half of what he writes, I don't understand. He won't clarify anything but when I don't do what he expects, he writes another email telling me that I blew it. He's driving me nuts!"

I suggest to Duane that he start communicating with Troy via email, since that's how Troy seems most comfortable dealing with his staff.

"But I don't have time to write a huge email to him!"

"Could you write him an email that says, 'Can we have lunch tomorrow?'"

"He'll say no."

I suggest he phrase it as "When would you be available to have lunch with me?" because it is unlikely Troy will reply "Never."

"Once you get him to commit to lunch," I tell Duane, "then you can prepare all the questions you want to ask him during that lunch."

Duane looks at his hands. "But I can't stand the guy. I don't want to have lunch with him."

"Duane, that's a completely different issue," I tell him.

· · ·

I point out that he has been putting more emotional energy into managing his feelings about Troy than into his job. He's tied in an emotional knot. To help him untangle the knot, I ask him a series of questions that will help him see the fix he is in.

"Duane, if you are unwilling to have lunch with Troy, why would Troy want to spend time with you?"

"He's the manager. He's supposed to be the one to reach out."

"Why?"

"Because that's what managers are supposed to do."

"And how long will you wait for him to reach out?"

"Until I get fed up and find another job."

"And what are you going to do when you run into another Troy at your next job?"

Now I have Duane's attention. "What is the absolute worst thing that could happen if you reached out to him instead?" I continue.

"I could lose my job."

"But you just told me you were willing to stay here until it got so bad that you left. How is that any different than losing your job?"

"He just pisses me off."

"Back to basics here, Duane. What's the only thing you can change?"

"I know, I know."

"When you are ready to see this from the position of what you can do differently, not how to change Troy, we can start to work. Will you let me know when you're ready?"

A long silence, then, "I'll call you."

. . .

Duane calls the very next day.

"I asked him to lunch," he reports. "The date's set for Wednesday."

"Great. What are you going to talk about?'

"I want to know why his door is closed all the time, and why he only sends emails instead of talking to me."

"Can you frame that into questions that won't make Troy feel defensive?"

Duane thinks about that for a few seconds.

"How about, 'Why is your door closed all the time?'"

"How do you think Troy will respond to that style of question?"

Duane agrees that maybe he should soften the question a bit more. "How about 'I noticed your door is closed a lot. Is that the way you like to work?'"

I agree that this phrasing is more neutral. "What else do you want to ask him?"

"Do you like to communicate via email as opposed to talking in person?"

"Duane, don't you already know the answer to that question?"

"Of course I do, but I need to make him understand that I don't like to communicate that way."

"Why not ask him a question that would help him come to that conclusion?"

"Have you noticed that I do not like to communicate via email?"

"That's leading, and a bit terse. Can you make it a bit more user-friendly?"

"How about, 'Troy, I think you and I prefer different forms of communication. You seem to prefer email. Do you know what I prefer?'"

"I think that works. Now let's think about his potential answers. When you ask him why his door is closed, he could say, 'Because I have attention-deficit disorder and I need complete focus to get my work done. I've tried years of experimenting and closing my door seems to work best for me.' What's your comeback if he says that?"

Duane looks thunderstruck. "I never thought of anything like that. That sort of changes the water on the minnows, doesn't it?"

"Duane, what is it that bugs you about his door being closed?" I ask.

"It makes me feel like he never has time to talk with me. He appears completely inaccessible."

"Can you ask Troy a question that will help him to consider how those around him feel when he keeps his door closed all day long?"

"Do you know the effect your closed door has on me?"

"That is very direct, and I think it will help Troy think about how his actions affect others. Now, think about the possible responses Troy could give you to that question."

"Well, he could say, 'Tough tootsie—that's the way I work.'"

"Do you really think that's how he'll respond?"

"No. He could say, 'I never thought about how my closed door affects anyone else.' Or, he could say, 'No, how does me keeping my door closed affect you?'"

"Great. Now you need to be prepared to explain how keeping his door closed affects you. Can you do that succinctly and objectively?"

"Yes."

"Good. Now, what are the possible answers to 'Do you know what my preferred style of communication is?'"

"I guess there are several, but the most honest one is probably 'No.' I can't imagine he has a clue about how I like to communicate. If he did, why would he rely on email all the time?"

"Duane, how can someone learn what your most favorite communication style is?"

"They just have to ask me!"

"What if they don't think to ask you?"

"I would just tell them!"

"Have you told Troy?"

"No. I was hoping he would ask."

· · ·

How often does this scene repeat itself in your company? How much emotional energy is wasted because no one asks questions?

Duane is a savvy marketing guy, highly paid and professional. But he can't get out of his own way and find a clear path to success. He needs to be reminded that his success depends on his ability to help others develop themselves, even if that means developing a supervisor! And the best way to develop someone is … by asking them questions.

When I coach, I suggest that my clients observe the 80/20 rule. Make sure that 80 percent of your conversations are interrogative. That means that 80 percent of the time you open your mouth, your sentences should end with question marks.

What do you think happens when I first ask my clients to do this?

The next time we meet, they are frustrated, even angry. They have a bunch of stories to share about sitting tongue-tied when they couldn't think of a question. They desperately wanted to *tell* the other person something, but to observe the 80/20 rule, they had to phrase it in the form of a question. It was like being caught in a perpetual game of *Jeopardy*!

Why is this so difficult? Because they have to *practice* asking questions!

Learning how to ask purposeful, powerful questions is a skill. Think about it. The first time you golfed, did you hit the ball long and straight? When you got behind the wheel of a car when you were 15½ years old, could you parallel park?

Probably not. Unless you're naturally gifted, it takes a certain amount of practice to learn how to golf and to master driving an automobile safely. And for everybody who isn't naturally gifted as a leader, it also takes time to learn how to ask the purposeful, powerful questions that you can use to develop your people.

THE CHALLENGE
Give the Benefit of the Doubt

As Duane's experience shows, giving someone the benefit of the doubt puts them in a place of comfort. They don't feel defensive. You get much better information and much better results.

For example, instead of asking, *Why do you keep your door closed all the time?*, you might say, *I've noticed that you like to work with your door closed. I hate to interrupt you, so can you tell me what would be a good way to let you know I need to talk with you?*

This may sound elementary, but it's not. If you don't believe me, try it. It sounds so easy when you are reading it in a book, but when real life is happening, emotions kick in and it is a completely different story. The best way to get good at asking questions that give the other person the benefit of the doubt is by practicing.

The following questions are phrased in a way that could easily put the person being questioned on the defensive. Your job is to rephrase them so that they are neutral and give the other person the benefit of the doubt. Take out a piece of paper and write neutral responses to these questions:

- *Why didn't you respond to my email?*

- *Where is that report I asked for last week?*

- *Why were you late for work again?*

- *Do you know what your numbers for next month will look like?*

FOR FURTHER CONSIDERATION

Here are some ways to reword hard questions to give a team member the benefit of the doubt:

ORIGINAL: *Why didn't you respond to my email?*
NEUTRAL: *I know you're busy. I was wondering if you had a chance to review my email regarding the XYZ Project?*

. . .

ORIGINAL: *Where is that report I asked for last week?*
NEUTRAL: *Remember that report I asked you for last week? Do you think I could have it today?*

. . .

ORIGINAL: *Why were you late for work again?*
NEUTRAL: *I've noticed you've been a little challenged getting here in a timely manner lately. Is there anything I can help with?*

. . .

ORIGINAL: *Do you know what your numbers for next month will look like?*
NEUTRAL: *I need the numbers for next month. When do you think you can get them to me?*

POSTSCRIPT

Duane puts a lot of emotional energy into changing his style. He starts asking lots of questions at work and he finds a great balance with his new boss. His future with the company is bright. He's now rated as a high-potential employee due to his leadership ability. He tells me that means he knows how to develop people.

I'm happy to report that Duane does not confine his new question-asking skills to the workplace. He takes them home to an overtaxed marriage that is on its way to divorce court. It isn't easy, but he and his wife are learning to ask each other a lot of questions. These questions lead to discussions that help them to understand each other in ways they never thought possible. (This spillover benefit isn't guaranteed to fix all troubled marriages, however!)

3
Prepare to Ask Questions

Human Resources calls to ask me to consider coaching Tim, the vice president of a $300 million business unit that's part of a $1 billion senior living conglomerate.

In order to get an objective point of view, I always do a miniature 360 before I meet with a potential client. I interview four direct reports and the person to whom the candidate reports.

When I speak with his four direct reports, I learn that Tim "over-delegates and micromanages." He gives his people a tremendous amount of work, and then tells them exactly how to accomplish it. One employee tells me, "Tim actually told me who to call on my way home that night, what to talk to them about, and to report the details of the conversation to him when I arrived at the office the next morning." And then he adds, "I run an $80 million dollar business division. I do not expect to be managed like this."

Yet another of Tim's direct reports tells me that Tim's expectations of her are constant perfection with no reward or recognition. He runs the business based on numbers, which is all that matters; people, he says, are easy to replace.

Another of Tim's direct reports tells me that the difference between reporting to Tim versus reporting to his last boss is the difference between coming to work in a good mood and not wanting to come to work at all.

Tim's boss, Bob, has a very different story to tell. He thinks Tim is a strong producer. The business he manages is in excellent fiscal health. He's always available when Bob needs answers. He feels he can depend on Tim, whose judgment he trusts.

After hearing Bob's report on Tim, I ask why Human Resources contacted me to coach Tim. Bob doesn't hesitate.

"Tim has only been in this position for eight months. And while the business is doing well, we've lost two good, high potential people. Their exit interviews reflected poorly on Tim. We can't totally trust those exit interviews because we believe both of those employees wanted Tim's job and were upset that they did not get it. Their anger toward Tim could be their reason for leaving the company. But it could also be Tim's style of management and leadership. The truth is we're not sure which it is, so we've decided to be proactive by getting Tim some support immediately."

"Have you spent any time talking with the people who report to Tim?" I ask.

"No. I haven't had the time."

"Do you have enough of a relationship with any of Tim's direct reports that they would open up to you and be honest?"

"Probably not. I'm relatively new in my position too."

It's time for me to meet Tim. But first, I prepare some questions.

. . .

Before a potentially hot meeting like this, I always brainstorm a list of questions that help me keep to the 80/20 rule. This first list consists of broad-based questions that I will follow with specific questions that I come up with on the spot, depending on the answers to the first questions.

I start with a good deal of "getting to know you" questions that include understanding the potential client's life and employment history. Although many would prefer to keep their personal and professional lives separate, there is no doubt in my mind that it matters if someone has survived divorce; the death of a parent, child or spouse; being fired; major health issues; or never finished college. Once those findings are complete, it is time to uncover your purpose. In this particular situation, the following questions are some of what I would use.

- *Why do you want an executive coach?*

- *Have you ever been coached before? If so, what was your experience?*

- *How would your people describe you?*

- *What do you presently do to develop your people?*

When it's your turn to come up with a First List, write down your questions and take the list with you to the meeting.

. . .

Tim is physically imposing. He is 6'4" and is on the husky side. He smiles as he reaches to shake my hand, tells me it's a pleasure to meet me. We exchange pleasantries and I start.

"Your Human Resources department called me and asked me to talk with you about being your executive coach. My first question for you is, do you want a coach, and if so, why?"

"I see having a coach as a great opportunity for me to learn more about myself. I had a coach once before but didn't really learn that much from her. I understand you have a particular style, sort of an 'in your face' kind of style. I think I'd like that better and would learn more from some one who gives it to me straight."

"What did you and your previous coach accomplish?"

"We talked a lot about the business, how it runs, how we could improve it."

"What did you learn about yourself during that coaching process?"

"I learned that I'm a straight shooter. Right to the point."

"Is that how your people would describe you?"

"They would probably say I am direct and to the point. They'd tell you that I am demanding and expect them to work hard. That I like the numbers to add up and I hold them accountable for that."

"Anything else?"

"They might say that this is good preparation for the opportunity to run a multi-million dollar business. Sort of, 'If I can work for this guy I can work for anyone' type attitude."

"Is that the way you want it to be?"

"What do you mean?"

"That thought you just shared with me—'If I can work for this guy I can work for anyone.' Is that the way you want it to be?"

"I have high standards."

"I'm not sure that answered my question."

"I guess I want it that way. I want them to feel accomplished every day. I want them to understand that their hard work pays off, that we can run a great business together."

"Do you think that's what your people are thinking right now?"

"I've only been here for eight months. I am not sure we've been together long enough to truly know what they're thinking."

"How long do you think you need to be together to find out?"

"I don't know."

"What do you know about your people, Tim?"

"I know that this is a very successful business that we've inherited. I know that we are lucky to have this opportunity to work in this division. I know that corporate respects us and at the same time expects great things from us."

"I asked you about your people. What do you know about your people?"

"I'm not sure what you're getting at?"

"What do you do to develop your people?"

"I spend time with them. We have lots of group meetings."

"Tim, what I am trying to understand is your interest in developing your people versus your interest in having the best numbers in the company. Given the choice, which would you want, the numbers or the people?"

Tim pauses for a moment, clearly thinking hard about this question.

"I guess I'd want the best numbers in the company. That's what really matters; this is business, isn't it? I want to keep my job."

I understand Tim's position. It's important to run a good business. What he doesn't seem to connect with is the importance of his people.

"Tell me about a mentor you've had in your business. Tell me about someone who really helped you understand how to run this business, someone you really enjoyed working with, someone who to this day stands out in your mind."

Tim thinks for a moment.

"I really don't have one. I can't think of anyone who has truly mentored me, or anyone who really taught me the business. I learned the hard way. I worked 70 hours a week and I always watched the numbers. I've had great opportunities, but I am not sure one person helped me find my way here."

Tim has never had anyone invest in him.

. . .

What types of questions come next? How can I help Tim see the importance of developing his people? Does he need to know how unhappy his team is?

I make another question list.

- *Does your team enjoy working for you?*

- *How do you know?*

- *What do you think they want from you?*

- *Are you willing to ask them?*

I write them down and take them with me to the next meeting.

"Tim, does your team enjoy working for you?"

"I sure hope so. If our numbers are any indication, they love working for me. I guess I haven't given it much thought."

"Do you like working for Bob?"

"Oh, Bob is great."

"Why?"

"Bob gives me a lot of rope. He lets me do my thing, and as long as my numbers are good, he leaves me alone. He calls when he needs something and we see each other at quarterly operations meetings. He is the perfect boss."

"Is that what your team would say about you?"

Tim thinks for a moment.

"I'm not sure. We've only been together for eight months."

"How long have you been reporting to Bob?"

"Eight months. But he knew me before this."

"As a direct report?"

"We've both worked here for over seven years. It's a fairly intimate organization and most of us know each other."

"Why can you say Bob is a perfect boss after eight months, but your people can't say the same thing about you after the same amount of time?"

"I guess I never thought of it that way."

"Do you think they'd like to be able to say that?"

"I don't know. But I know I'd like to hear it."

"What do you think your team wants from you?"

"I guess I'm not really sure."

"Would it help you do your job if you knew more about what they wanted?"

"Of course it would."

"Are you willing to ask them?"

"Ask them what they want from me? That seems odd. I can't imagine what they'd say."

"How can we find out?"

"I guess I'd have to ask them."

. . .

In my work there are questions that always work for me, questions I can lean on at any given time. Tim and I talk about how he, as a leader, could put together his own list. Our ideas are very different.

He suggests that an anonymous survey of his four direct reports would give him the best feedback.

I want him to talk individually with each member of his team, but I'm worried that he might not be able to do that as objectively as it needed. We go with the survey.

Here's what Tim learned about how his team sees him:

- Tim is combative, not collaborative.

- He does not value the individual.

- Tim does not trust us.

- He runs this business based on fear of bad results.

- I am looking for another job either within or outside this company.

"What do you think?" I ask Tim.

"Pretty dismal," he replies.

THE CHALLENGE
Make a List of "First Questions"

Here's a challenge one leader faces. As you read the story, think what your own "first questions" list would look like.

Scott is a senior vice president of sales. He has a great team except for his finance professional, Kirk. Scott inherited Kirk; he did not hire him on his own. Kirk is a numbers guy, but he lacks creativity. Scott is frustrated. He needs Kirk to bring him information that goes above and beyond weekly reports to interpret trends and predict likely outcomes. Scott doesn't know *how* to manipulate the numbers; he came up through the sales ranks, and besides, he isn't supposed to know how to do this. Scott's peers all have finance professionals who give them all sorts of nifty financial information.

Kirk thinks he's doing his job just fine. Scott hasn't been able to get Kirk to understand what he wants. If you were Scott, what questions would you ask Kirk to help him understand what you wanted? Take out a piece of paper and write them down. Trust me, it is more effective if you write them down.

FOR FURTHER CONSIDERATION
Here are non-threatening statements to prepare and questions to get ready for the difficult meeting with Kirk.

- *Kirk, I appreciate the job you do with the weekly reports; they are always correct and timely. I'm wondering what else we could do with these numbers?*

STOP TELLING. START ASKING.

- *Is there a picture these numbers paint that I don't see and maybe you do?*

- *I have a copy of a report that Larry Smith did for the Marketing group. It shows what's in our pipeline versus how many deals we close. Do you know how he did this? If not, could you talk with Larry and find out what spreadsheet he uses?*

- *Can you get creative and try to find what else our numbers tell us?*

- *Kirk, I am not a finance guy, that's why I have you. Do you understand what it is I need from you?* If Kirk says yes, follow up with this: *Great! Tell me what you think I need so we're sure we're on the same page.*

Now try it with your situation. Make a list of questions.

When you think about your work situation, what is the first challenge that comes to your mind? Write it down.

Make a list of everyone who could potentially be involved in this challenge.

Write their names next to the challenge.

Now come up with three questions you would like to ask each of these people. Remember to write the questions giving them the benefit of the doubt. Write questions that allow them to think rather than feeling on the defensive.

Once you have a list of questions, you can prepare to take action. Plan your course of action first. Meet with each person on your list in a one-on-one setting to ask your questions. Note: it's important to do this one-on-one; this will not work in a group setting because the dynamics of a one-on-one setting are infinitely different than a group setting. In a one-on-one setting you can more easily

- Watch body language

- Control the silence. If you are not talking, the only other person talking is the one you want to be talking

- Have complete accountability. A group setting dilutes accountability

POSTSCRIPT

Tim and I work together for six months, meeting for 90 minutes every other week. We focus on one thing: developing his ability to ask questions.

Tim struggles with the 80/20 rule. Often he gets frustrated and just tells his team what to do. He sees the value of the question but does not always have the patience to work on finding the right one. He continues to try.

He loses two more members of his team during those six months. He still runs a very successful division and is considered a leader in the corporation, but his name has been taken off the list of candidates who are in line for succession to more senior positions.

4

Be Brave Enough to Ask
the Hard Questions

Brian started his own practice after several years with a large New York advertising firm. He had been frustrated with the internal politics of a large firm and wanted to build a place where the creative people spend their time helping clients rather than meeting to discuss how to run the partnership, a place where they would not have to think about administrative issues. The terms of the partnership agreement spell this out clearly for every ad executive who joins the new firm.

"I am the majority stockholder," Brian tells me. "There are five other partners, none of whom own more than 5 percent of the firm. Each advertising executive gets paid an annual salary that is lower than the market average, but they also receive annual bonuses that are higher than the market. The system operates like golden handcuffs; they won't leave while waiting for their annual bonus."

In addition to running the firm, Brian has a thriving advertising clientele of his own. He specializes in entertainment advertising and has a client list any advertising firm would die for. He comes to work at five in the morning, a short commute from his Manhattan penthouse, and leaves around four in the afternoon. He hires Walter a few years after he starts the firm and sells 13 percent of the firm to him. Walter clearly is Brian's hand-picked successor, a decision that involves no one but Brian.

· · ·

My first contact with this advertising agency does not come through Brian. It comes in the form of a brief call from Joyce, the director of administration of the firm. She asks me to come to the office to meet with Brian and her.

The office is a class B space. The carpet is a bit worn in spots, the artwork is outdated, and the conference room needs more windows. The receptionist is friendly. Before she calls Joyce's office, she tells me I will be meeting first with Joyce, who turns out to be warm and engaging.

"So what seems to be the challenge here?" I ask as soon as the pleasantries are concluded.

"Morale," she replies without hesitation. "I can't put my finger on it, but there is an overwhelming sense of dissatisfaction here. I notice our executives rolling their eyes when I ask things of them. There is no camaraderie, no feeling that we are all in this together. When someone has a great win, when we bring in a new client or win an award, we don't celebrate, even if I suggest it.

"And just so you know, it was my idea to contact you, not Brian's. He doesn't seem to think anything is wrong."

"How are your relationships with the partners and other employees?" I ask.

"Some good, some not so good. I came out of the military. I don't have a advertising background, and they all know it. I don't think five years at sea with the navy matters to this group, even though I earned my bachelor's degree when I left the navy. Some of them think of me as overhead; they don't value my work or my input. Others see me as Brian's hired gun."

"Are you?"

"No."

"Then what are you?"

Joyce laughs at my question, clearly because she thinks it's funny—but I also sense that she's hoping that laughing will get her out of answering my question. I maintain eye contact, and wait.

"I run the office," she says finally. "I choose our health insurance provider. I hire the assistants, receptionist, artistic folks, and the ad executives. I do payroll. I make sure the copy machines are working, the refrigerator is stocked and the cleaning people do their job. I guess I do everything except create ads."

"Who do the partners think you work for?"

"Probably for Brian, but they're wrong. I work for the firm."

"Tell me about your relationship with Brian."

"We've been working together for three years. We know each other pretty well. I know when's a good time to approach him with something, and I know when I need to wait an hour, a day, or even a week. He can be volatile."

"Does he know that?"

"That he's volatile?"

I nod my head.

"I guess so, although it isn't something he'd readily admit. He's tried to build a different kind of advertising firm here. He wants the firm to be a place where you can be wildly successful and not have to deal with any of the day-to-day hassles of managing an ad agency. We have one partner meeting a year in which Brian gives a state-of-the-firm speech. That's it. But it just seems that we need more."

"More what?"

"More time *together*," she says. "More time to have fun together, more time to celebrate our successes. The way we do it, it is all about the W-2. Nothing else seems to matter. We are creative people, we should know how to create a celebration."

It's time for me to meet Brian.

· · ·

He's 5'7", with a full head of hair and a mean handshake. He appears to be in great shape. His office, overlooking the south end of the Hudson River, would have been large even if he'd been managing partner of Leo Burnett. Given that his firm has five partners, not a hundred, it is downright enormous.

We get right to business.

"Joyce seems to think the firm lacks camaraderie," I tell him. "Do you agree?"

He leans back in his chair.

"That depends on your definition of camaraderie. Financially, we are wildly successful, and isn't that why most of us come to work? We have to pay the bills."

"That's certainly one reason we all go to work," I agree. "Are there reasons besides money that people work?"

"None that matter," Brian says. "We can talk about being a part of a team or talk about doing good deeds for the world, but the truth is, we work to earn money, don't we? Don't you?"

I let that comment sit; I am not ready to have that discussion quite yet. I redirect the conversation.

"Who makes the decisions at this firm?"

"Mostly me, sometimes Joyce. It depends on the magnitude of the decision."

"Do your partners ever get involved in the workings of the firm?"

"Not really. I make that very clear when I hire them."

"How did you explain it to them during the hiring process?" I ask. "What did you say that helped them understand how it all works here?"

"I told them I started this firm to get away from being meeting-ed to death like I was at ad agencies where I'd worked in the past. I wanted to build a firm where creative people could create and have someone else run the firm. I was very clear with each of them during the hiring process."

"Do you ever ask for their input?"

"Nope."

"Do they ever give you unsolicited input?"

"Not if I can help it."

"Do you want anything here to be different, or are you happy with the way things are?"

"I think things are fine. Look at the numbers! We're doing great. We billed $44.2 million last year. I won't divulge our profit margins, but they'd make every other firm in town look like mom-and-pop operations."

"Did you know that Joyce was bringing me in to talk about the lack of camaraderie here?

"She told me she was bringing in a consultant to help her do her job better, to be a sort of coach for her. I said let me know how much it costs and I'll tell you if you can do it."

"Brian, why don't you want to have meetings with your partners?"

"It's a waste of time."

"Do you think you could survive working in an advertising agency where all you did was sell and create advertising and you had nothing to say in how the firm was run?"

"As long as it was run the way I wanted it to be run, I'd be fine."

"Do you think you're running this firm the way your partners want it run?"

"Yes. I think they are all pretty happy doing their thing and taking home their bonuses at the end of the year. It's not perfect, but I've yet to find a firm that is."

"What would be the harm in asking for their input?"

"I don't need it. I know how to run this firm, and they know how to sell and create advertising."

He thinks about this briefly, steepling his fingers. Then he leans forward in his chair, hands on his desk.

"The truth is, I don't want to know what they have to say. I want them to go be productive advertising people."

"Would you mind if I talked with a few of your employees? If they're unhappy with the level of camaraderie, I can gauge it from them. There's no charge for my services until I believe I can help you, and I am not there yet."

"As long as we're not paying you, you can talk to anyone you want!"

We both smile. I shake his hand and thank him for his time.

. . .

My next step is to meet a each of the five partners and get their thoughts on how perfect or not perfect the firm is. I ask Joyce if I could contact them directly.

"You can," she says, "but they might not speak to you. It would probably be better if I asked a few of them to meet with you. I'll explain what we are trying to do."

I think about asking Joyce why that is, but decide to wait. I can ask the partners instead.

Joyce sets up individual thirty-minute meetings with the five partners. We meet in the conference room at the firm.

Here's what I learn:

The firm has a camaraderie challenge, all right, but not the one Joyce thinks. The challenge is between the ad executives and the Brian-Joyce-Walter team. The camaraderie among the rest of the executives and employees is strong because they've all bonded very well—against Brian.

Each of them tells me Brian was clear when he hired them: there would be no meetings. They could just be advertising executives. It had sounded great at the time, but they hadn't realized that it meant they would have no say in simple things, such as what cell phone plan they'd use, which artistic assistant they worked with, how much of the firm's money Brian spent on art, or—the biggest sticking point of them all—how the annual bonus was calculated.

The partners all know their annual earnings are roughly 5 percent higher than the average, but that was attractive only during the first few years. Now, it doesn't seem to be a factor in their collective dissatisfaction.

One partner tells me: "In most advertising agencies, the senior people help the junior people develop their clientele. The senior person takes them under their wing, invites them to trade events now and then and to dinner with one of their clients. They talk with each other and learn from each other. The mentor observes the junior person's work and client relationships and gives feedback, or they invite the junior to observe them at client meetings in order to learn from them. They bring the younger staff in on key decisions about their own careers and maybe even the firm's future direction. We've all seen the television show *Mad Men*, that's how it works.

"None of that happens here. Here, it's just 'You eat what you kill.' But even in the wild, the mom teaches the young to survive."

The relationship between Brian and the five partners is broken, possibly beyond repair. Brian hasn't a clue that the real reason they don't talk with him is not because he doesn't solicit their opinion. It's because they can't stand him, and all five agree that the reason no one wanted to talk with me is fear of retribution.

"If Brian finds out what we said, it could affect our bonuses," one tells me. They confess that they agreed to talk with me only on the condition that I do not share any specific comments with Brian that might identify them. They only went along with the interview because they had talked among themselves and agreed that it was time to let Brian know how they felt.

I ask them about Joyce. Where does she fit in?

"She's a good person, but what Brian says, goes. She follows his orders. A lot of the time she tries to make things better, but she's between a rock and a hard place and is too used to saluting to stand up to Brian. It must be difficult to be in her position."

I end each of my meetings with the same question: *Why do you stay if you dislike it so much?*

Each partner says more or less the same thing: "Finding a new place to work takes a lot of time. We have plenty of work here, and we're very busy. When things slow down, we might go looking, or we might all leave together and start our own firm."

. . .

Since Joyce is my main contact, I decide to circle back to her.

"Would it surprise you to know that you have a major challenge at this firm?" I ask.

She puts her head in her hands.

"Be careful what you wish for," she mumbles. Then she lifts her head and tells me to give it to her straight.

I share the common threads from my discussions with the partners. I ask why she and Brian are so reluctant to ask them for their input. She looks at me, clearly surprised.

"Me, too? It's not just Brian? They don't like either of us?"

"It's not a matter of *liking*," I say. "They see you as an extension of Brian. They perceive that you can't do much without his okay."

Joyce nods. She had been prepared to hear the feedback about Brian, but it's clear it pains her to realize that she's also part of the challenge.

"Where do we go from here?" she asks.

"We go to Brian and ask him if he has any interest in making things different."

Joyce lets out a big sigh. "Yeah, right."

. . .

Joyce chooses not to take part in my meeting with Brian. She says he will listen better and dial down the bravado if she's not there.

"Your partners are unhappy," I tell Brian. "They want more of a say in decision-making. They want a chance to voice their opinions. The lack of control frustrates them."

Brian shakes his head and smiles. "Then why don't they leave?"

"They haven't yet reached their breaking point."

Brian is still smiling. "When will they?"

"I don't know."

"I'll take my chances," Brian says. Meeting over.

I go back to Joyce and give her a word-by-word report of my meeting with Brian. She grimaces.

"What am I supposed to do?"

"I see only two good choices," I say. "You can stay here and try to effect change between Brian and the team. Or, you can leave."

"I'll never find a job that pays what Brian pays, and I like my work. With my military retirement, I'm doing pretty well for myself."

"There's a third option, but I don't think you'll like it. It's playing ostrich: you put your head in the sand and continue as you were."

She drums her fingers on her desk.

"I got everyone's hopes up. Now I can't deliver. I told them you were going to help us learn to work better as a team."

"Joyce, when you told them that, what did they say?

"Most of them laughed."

. . .

Brian doesn't engage his staff because he does not want to hear their answers. Deep down he knows they would tell him exactly what he does not want to hear. He prefers to operate in a bubble.

On the Friday before Labor Day of the following year, three of the firm's partners quit to start a competing advertising agency. They give notice in the middle of the afternoon—to Walter, the 13-percent owner, rather than Brian. They clean out their desks, and walk out of the door with $16 million of the firm's $44.2 million billings.

When Joyce asks for a forwarding address and telephone number, one of the exiting partners hands her a business card with the new firm's address, phone number, and email and website addresses. They have been planning this for months.

The partners leave because Brian is unwilling to help them grow in their careers. He refuses to involve them in decision-making, to introduce them to new clients, to help them build their book of business (which would only benefit the firm), or to be a mentor.

Once they get over getting a big paycheck, the partnerss realize they hate being treated like part of the overhead. They want a say in their working conditions. Most of all, they want to be a part of a advertising team, not an advertising assembly line.

Brian's response?

"I can't believe they didn't at least talk with me! They just walked out the door without ever giving me a chance. How was I supposed to know they weren't happy?"

· · ·

I decide to visit with Joyce one more time. Brian is not coachable. But Joyce might be.

· · ·

"Joyce, if you want things to change around here, where do you think it could start?

"I think if we had meetings and did stuff together it would help. Maybe a day or two of teambuilding?"

"Do you really think that's what this firm needs?

She stares at me.

"Joyce, if you want change, I'm afraid it needs to start with you."

"Why me?"

"Because Brian trusts you and Brian confides in you. If you start asking him some hard questions, he has no choice but to see that it can be different."

"What do you want me to ask him?"

"Ask him if he really wants to rebuild a firm where no one has any say in the operations of the firm."

"He will say yes."

"Ask him if he really wants to have to build the firm over, again and again, because people seem to eventually get fed up with this system."

"I can't do that. He might fire me. That questions might cause irreparable harm to our relationship. I cannot take that risk."

"Is that what you want, Joyce? Can you stay here and watch it happen all over again?"

"I told you before, I could never make the money Brian pays me elsewhere. I have about ten years until I retire. I just don't want to make waves right now, especially in light of the walkout we just experienced. I know that sounds weak, but it's the right decision for me."

. . .

The number one reason most people enjoy their work is because they are a part of something positive that is bigger than themselves. When one car headlight burns on its own, it illuminates 500 feet ahead of the car. When both headlights are operating, the distance that's illuminated is 800 feet. It is all about the synergy.

Brian thinks that he treats the partners in his firm very well, and that making decisions for them will work because it is what he wants from his career. He wants a happy stable of low-maintenance advertising executives who make money for the firm and money for themselves.

Unfortunately for Brian, most of the people he hired eventually determined that the golden handcuffs are more handcuff than golden. After they get their bearings, they find they are not content with the equivalent of punching a time-clock and stamping out advertising sales and advertising creativity in a vacuum. They want to learn and grow and be successful together as a team. They will be, but not with Brian.

. . .

Most people are reluctant to ask questions because they don't want to hear the answer. Did your mother ever ask you if she was a good mom? How many teachers have asked you how they did, if they presented material in such a way that you could comprehend it, if you enjoyed their class?

Most people will tell you it's just human nature to avoid things you don't want to hear, so consider yourself forewarned. This book is all about overcoming human nature. If you want to improve your ability to develop people, you're going to have to take a deep breath and learn to ask the questions that really need to be asked.

Can you recall a time early in your career when you wanted to know whether your boss thought you were doing a good job? A time when you felt on shaky ground and wondered how you measured up to expectations?

You probably never asked, because you weren't sure what the answer was going to be, and there was one answer you really didn't want to hear—the one that said you were under-performing and that your job was in jeopardy.

What would have been different in your life if you had asked that question? Would your work product have changed? Would your focus have changed? Would the amount of emotional energy you were using just to wonder about the situation have changed? Was hearing that you were doing a great job (or a mediocre job, or lousy job) *really* what mattered?

I doubt it. I think what truly would have mattered is that you would finally *know*.

Without asking the un-askable questions, you live in the world of an eternal "I don't know." And in that world, you spend enormous amounts of emotional energy on feeling insecure because you wonder what the truth is.

So why not ask?

THE CHALLENGE
How to Ask the Hard Questions

You are the global vice president of sales for a $500 million company. One of your most productive district managers, Wayne, has hired his son, Trevor, to be the office assistant. Trevor does not report to Wayne but to Barb, the office manager. Both Wayne and Barb report to you.

At first, this setup seemed to work, but more recently there have been complaints from other employees regarding Trevor. Barb is the recipient of these complaints, and she brings them to you. Apparently Trevor comes to work late, takes long lunches, and leaves early. He gets his dad's work done but doesn't contribute to the rest of the team. When Barb attempts to talk with him, he goes to Dad for help. When this happens, Wayne goes to Barb to smooth things out.

Take out a piece of paper and write down answers to the following questions:

- *What questions would you ask Wayne?*
- *What questions would you ask Barb?*
- *What questions would you ask Trevor?*

FOR FURTHER CONSIDERATION

Questions for Wayne

- *How is Trevor working out in the office?*

- If he says good, ask: *Would the staff share your thoughts?*

- If he says bad, ask: *How do you think we can address this challenge?*

- *Tell me your thoughts on the challenges of hiring family?*

- *Are you facing any of those challenges?*

Questions for Barb

- *How is Trevor performing as the office assistant?*

- *Have you shared these thoughts with Trevor?*

- *Do you have any thoughts regarding what you might do to affect his performance?*

- *Given the choice, would you have hired Trevor?*

- *Without me doing your job or putting you in a difficult position, how can I help you?*

Questions for Trevor

I would not question Trevor.

You spending time developing Trevor is not the message you want to send to your team. You are developing Wayne and Barb to deal with this situation. They need to find a way to solution.

POSTSCRIPT

One of the most important aspects of being an executive coach is to know when to walk away from situations where you cannot be successful.

Brian is a great advertising executive. Brian is not coachable. I do not believe anything I say or do will influence him to change his approach. He begins the process of rebuilding his firm in exactly the same manner as he built in the first place. As of the day this book goes to print, he has four partners on staff. Joyce continues to work with Brian.

5

Drop Your Agenda

I walk into Suzie's office at two o'clock on a Tuesday afternoon. The office is bustling like a mall on the Saturday before Christmas. Phones ring, fax machines beep, copiers hum.

When I meet Suzie, I find she is five feet nothing, with short salt and pepper hair and blue eyes that twinkle. I like her immediately. She's dressed in business casual except for her shoes, which are open-toed Birkenstock sandals. She catches me taking them in.

"These are the only shoes I can wear," she tells me. "My feet are a mess."

I nod as if I understand what it means to have messed-up feet.

Suzie steers me into a small conference room. As I move to close the door, Suzie asks that I leave the door open, just a crack, just in case.

In case of what?

She reads my mind.

"In case someone needs me for something."

I begin to ask the usual questions about her business and her life, the basic ice-breaking, nonthreatening fact-finding questions that I use to start all first meetings with a new client. Her answers are short and I detect no reflection in her answers. Either she doesn't have the time to tell me the whole story, or she doesn't want me to know the whole story.

I'm going to have to slow her down if this conversation is going to work.

"Are you in a rush?" I ask.

"I live in a rush. If you don't move fast, you can't be successful in the real estate business."

"Do you like it like that?"

"Like what?"

"Do you like living in a rush?"

"No, I hate it! That's why I called you. I want to build my team so I can delegate more to them. I'm tired of doing it all by myself. The trouble is, they don't seem to want to work as hard as I do."

"How long has it been like this?"

Suzie laughs.

"I've been in this business for almost thirty years, so I guess that's how long. But I'm getting older. I want some time for myself, and my team doesn't seem to get it. I want you to light a fire under them so they'll start producing."

At this point I have three choices. I can begin to work with Suzy and help her learn the art of asking questions, I can meet the team and get a better understanding of the bigger picture, or I can do both.

I decide to do both.

I first meet with each team member one-on-one so I can understand each of them as individuals before I meet them as a group. Everyone is cooperative except Suzie's assistant, Cynthia, who tells me she's too busy to meet with me.

I call Suzie about this.

Cynthia suddenly finds a half hour to meet with me.

Two questions I make sure to ask each person are "How would you describe Suzie?" and "What's it like working with her?" Here is a sampling of the comments from the agents on Suzie's team:

"Suzie is amazing. There is no one like her in this town, probably not even this state. She works her butt off. The team is great. We all get along really well."

"Suzie lists more properties in a week than most real estate agents list in a year. I wish I knew how she does it. But she doesn't seem to have much time to teach me."

"Suzie is awesome. I love working with her. I wish I could spend more time with her, but she always seems unavailable, I guess because she's so busy doing deals. She does so many deals!"

"I'm proud to be part of this team. I am so new at the business I can't believe she took me on. I don't see her much except Monday morning meetings, but I love having her name on my business card. I've been trying to get to know the team better, because I'm scared that when it finally comes time to write an offer, I won't have anyone to help me walk through my first one."

Cynthia's comments are even more positive about Suzie, whom she clearly thinks is a very good person poorly served by her real estate team.

Suzie and I plan to meet one hour before the Monday staff meeting. She arrives thirty minutes late, barking orders to her support staff as she walks in the door.

"Did you remember that we were meeting this morning?" I ask.

"Yes," she says. "But I got tied up at a breakfast meeting and couldn't break away. Just let me tell Cynthia a few more things and I'll be ready to go."

I wait. By the time we are alone together in a closed-door office, the team meeting is ten minutes away from starting.

"Suzie, do you usually run this far behind schedule?"

"I'd like to say no, but the truth is, my schedule is a mess and I'm often late."

"We need to reschedule our conversation. But I'd like to give you one thing to work on during your staff meeting if you're willing to try something."

"Sure."

"I want you to ask a lot of questions."

"That's it?"

"See, you're already good at it."

The team meeting takes place in a large conference room that hasn't been redecorated since 1980. The burlap wall cloth is curling at the edges and the parquet floor desperately needs attention. The rectangular conference table is barely large enough to seat the ten women and two men on the team; some of them hug the corners. I sense a camaraderie among the team; there was more friendly chatter than I expected to see on a Monday morning. The seat at the head of the table remains vacant for ten minutes until Suzie bustles in.

"Sorry," she says, but she doesn't sound especially apologetic. "I was on the phone with Allen Jonas, the president of Standard Tile. I am working with him and his wife to sell his house and find him one somewhere between the 6000 and the 9000 block of Lake Drive."

She rolls her eyes. It's clear to the group that she's frustrated with this client and that the Jonases are difficult customers. It also appears that she thinks this justifies wasting, cumulatively, two hours of her team's time.

Studying papers in front of her and without looking up at any of the team members, Suzie says, "I hope everyone had a great weekend."

Silence from the other twelve people around table.

The purpose of the weekly meeting, according to what Suzie told me the previous week, is to discuss existing inventory, potential buyers, and any listings expected to come on the market this week. She turns to Sean and points her finger at him.

"How did your open house on East Bay Point go?"

"Overall, it was better than I expected. Six people came through, but I think two were just nosy neighbors. The Vikings game being delayed didn't help. No offers yet."

Suzie nods. She continues looking at the papers in front of her while Sean talks, finally looking up when he finishes.

"Who else had an open house yesterday?"

Several of the team members give similar reports. Some lament the effect of the Green Bay Packers' schedule; some say it had no effect on their open houses. One team member mentions that the seller on Lincoln Avenue needs to get his dogs out of the house if there's going to be another open house at that location, because the dogs are noisy and they smell.

Suzie takes no notes on any of the comments. She makes no suggestions about overcoming the Packer effect or how to tactfully defuse the dog situation.

Suzie turns in her chair and points at Sheila.

"Did you get a price reduction from the sellers on Hilton Way?" she asks.

Sheila replies that the sellers are out of the country.

"Do you have their cell number?"

"Yes, but they're on vacation in Mexico so I really did not want to interrupt them."

Suzie nods but gives no verbal feedback. She opens a thick black binder on the table in front of her. The entire team opens their black binders at the same time. Suzie pages through the binder, calling out street names.

"Acacia?"

While the broker in charge of this listing responds, Suzie is already turning to the next page.

"Clearwater?"

Becky has this listing. She lets out a big sigh and said, "No activity."

"Hilton Way?"

"Trying to get a price reduction," mumbles Sheila.

"Kent Parkway?"

"We have an offer on Kent," says another broker. "It's contingent upon financing and a house inspection. I do not think either will be a problem."

Suzie smiles at the broker with the good news. "When do you think they'll close?"

"May, at the latest. It's a divorce situation; the sellers really want to get it done."

Suzie continues through the binder. It is clear she expects quick, to-the-point answers. She ends with a house on Wallace Way. The agent in charge tells her they had a great open house and there is a good possibility an offer will come today.

Suzie nods. "Okay, any questions?"

She waits three seconds, and when no one says anything, stands and says "Thanks for your time." The meeting has ended as abruptly as it began.

Cynthia stands at the door, indicating via hand signals that Suzie needs to take a phone call. As Suzie leaves the meeting, she turns to me.

"Can you stick around for a few minutes, I'd like to talk to you."

I nod. There are a lot of things wrong with the way Suzie handled the meeting: her body language, her manner of addressing the staff, her lack of involvement in finding solutions to the problems they presented. But her style is only a symptom of a deeper issue: her broken relationship with her team. Until that is fixed, nothing will change.

As I wait for Suzie, I notice several team members hovering around her office door, clearly waiting for a word with her.

Unfortunately, once she's off the phone, none of them get her attention because she wants to talk with me.

We sit in her office, the door completely closed this time. We are not alone, however. Cynthia is at her desk in the far corner.

"How did that team meeting go?" I ask.

"Fairly typical," she responds. "I asked a lot of questions, just like you told me to, but I didn't get many answers. Except for Liz and Sean, I'm not sure what the rest of them are doing. Judy is new and I have high hopes for her, but I don't think many of them realize how hard you have to work to be successful in this business. I don't know how to get that message to them. Truthfully, I am not sure how I would hold this all together if I didn't have my assistant."

Cynthia continues her work as if we are not present.

"Cynthia does everything. She knows every listing we have, makes sure we are ready for every closing, even makes sure the copy machine works. She does so much for the people on this team and I don't think they properly appreciate her."

"Do you think the team members see Cynthia the same way you see her?"

Suzie tenses, apparently uncomfortable with the direction the conversation has taken. I wonder if it's because Cynthia is in the room.

"If they really thought about it, they would," she says.

I tell Suzie I have some thinking to do and that we will meet again in two weeks. I ask her to walk me to the front door. She looks startled. She clearly expected our conversation to continue. I get up, put on my coat, and she follows me out the door.

When Suzie and I are alone in the stairwell, I ask, "How would your team describe Cynthia?"

"They would tell you she is a very dedicated employee who is always there for me, always ready to go the extra mile, always able to stay late when I need her. They would probably see her as a model employee. I wish they all would work as hard as she does."

"I hear you telling me how she serves you, but not the team."

Suzie pauses for a moment, wrinkling her brow.

"When they need to know where I am, she lets them know," she says. "When they need to have information about a listing or an open house, she tells them. I guess she serves the team by giving them information."

"Can you think of any way in which Cynthia might work against the team?"

"Well, she can be a bit of a mother hen when it comes to me and to my schedule. Sometimes she complains about the team members. I know she thinks they're all lazy, that they don't help out as much as they should. But I know she does it just to protect me."

"You need protection from your own team?"

Suzie's brow grows more furrowed. She looks away from me.

"I never thought about it quite like that," she mutters.

"What was your agenda for that meeting?"

"Basic update: go through inventory and learn what's moving and what's not. It's a chance for the whole team to get together and discuss our work."

"Do you think that's what happened?

Suzie looks puzzled.

"I'd like you to be aware of a few things in the next two weeks. Are you willing?"

"What do you want me to do?"

"First, pay attention to Cynthia."

"What do you mean?"

"Pay attention to the way she speaks to your team members, her side comments, and how often she feeds your ego. But do not discuss any of your observations with her. Save them for our next meeting. Can you do that?"

I can tell this is not where Suzie expected my coaching to take us. She is expecting me to beat up the team for not working hard enough, and then work on changing the team, not her.

"And the other thing I want you to observe is the amount of time you spend with each team member individually. I would like you to keep a time log. Note which team member you were with, the purpose of your time together, and the length of time you spent together. Can you do that?"

She says she can.

· · ·

In order to ask questions that help others, you must first drop your agenda. If you're already convinced that your team is lazy, how can any question you ask help develop them? What would have been different in that meeting if Suzie had dropped her agenda before she started?

- When she asked her team members if they had a good weekend, she might have looked at them and waited for an answer.

- She might have facilitated a discussion regarding the smelly-dog problem.

- She might have asked Sheila if she thought it made sense to interrupt a vacation to get a price reduction.

- She wouldn't have pointed at each of them as if she were a principal scolding naughty school kids

- She would have looked at them when they were talking!

Dropping your agenda does not mean having no judgment. All it means is leaving those judgments at the door and focusing on asking quality questions for those around you in order to help them learn.

· · ·

When Suzie and I meet two weeks later, she is on time and well prepared. Initially I don't get a chance to discuss Suzie's need to drop her agenda. She is ready to unload.

"Cynthia is a problem," she starts out. "She treats the team members like second-class citizens. She mimics them behind their backs, purposely puts them on extended telephone hold, and gives them the third degree when they want to talk with me. I can't believe I never noticed this before. She's mean!"

Suzie has figured it out on her own.

"I have to talk to her," she goes on. "She cannot continue behaving so unprofessionally. But how am I going to have this conversation?"

"Remember when I asked you to ask questions in your staff meeting? You didn't do a very good job. Why not?"

"Because I thought the team was a bunch of lazy butts who weren't pulling their weight. I could barely look at them, let alone ask them questions. But now I see that I've been kept away from them. How did I get sucked in like this?" Suzie is livid. "I have to tell Cynthia this must stop."

"Do you think telling her to stop will solve the problem?"

"It better, or I'll fire her."

"Suzie, are you willing to try asking some more questions?"

"Like what? *Cynthia, why are you so mean to my team?*"

"Suzie, that's the first time I've heard you refer to them as your team. When your agenda was that the team was lazy and needed to work harder, you referred to them as the team. Not your team."

"They *are* my team, damn it. And I want to know why she's so mean to them."

"Do you think she'd be able to answer that honestly, or would she get defensive?"

"She'd get defensive. Let's rethink this."

"Try to find a question that would put the dilemma in Cynthia's mind, help her to understand what you are seeing. Help her to learn what you've learned, that you've been serving one agenda. What could you ask her?"

"I think I'd ask her if she likes the members of my team. She'd be lying if she said anything but no."

"What if she says she doesn't like them? What would you ask next?"

"I'd ask her why she works here."

"And what if she says she works here because she likes working with you?"

"That's not enough! How can I build a team if my assistant treats them like crap?"

"Suzie, drop the agenda of being angry with Cynthia. Focus on what matters: building a successful team. What question can you ask Cynthia to help her understand how important that is to you?"

Suzie takes a deep breath. "Cynthia, how do you think I feel about the team?"

"Good. What do you think she'd say?"

"She might say that I think they are a bunch of lazy butts because she's heard me say that before.

"Is Cynthia a part of the team?"

"I guess I haven't treated her that way, but conceptually, yes, she is part of the team.

"Does she think she's part of your team?

"I don't know, but I think we'd better discuss it." Suzie pauses, looks at me and says, "How the hell did this happen?"

We both are quiet.

"Did you get caught up in your agenda?

"You mean I caused this?"

"You didn't prevent it."

· · ·

Before Suzie has her conversation with Cynthia she prepares four great questions.

1. Do you like my team?

2. Are you a part of my team?

3. Why are you not a part of my team?

4. What do you want your role to be here?

Together we consider every turn the conversation could take. We role-play every angle. Finally, she feels ready.

. . .

"How'd it go?" I ask when she calls to report the results.

"Not well. She does not want to be a part of the team—she wants to be my assistant. She thinks I picked the wrong people and that I should find new team members if I want better attitudes. She said she treats the team members the same way I do…like the lazy butts they are."

"What did you say?"

"I told her I made a huge mistake. That I realized, after looking at that time log you made me keep, that I don't spend much time with my team members. I speak unkindly about them, don't listen to them, and have not been a good leader for the team. She told me I was wrong, that I've busted my butt to try to help them and they were ungrateful. But when I asked her for an example, she didn't have one."

She pauses for what seems like a full minute.

"I need to change a lot of things around here."

"What do you need to change?"

"I need to spend time with my team members. When I was starting in the business, I had a great mentor. He took me everywhere he went, and I learned just from being with him. I am going to start spending one day each week with one of my team members. I'm going to quit thinking of them as lazy. I'm going to stop having an agenda and learn. I'm going to help them develop into great real estate professionals if that's what they want. I know it's what I want!"

THE CHALLENGE
How to Make Sure You are Dropping Your Agenda

Keith and Drew are partners in a small firm. They realize they are not getting along well enough to take the firm to the next level. Something needs to change: maybe one needs to buy the other one out; maybe they need to sell the business.

If you were Keith, what questions would you ask that would help both you and Drew to drop your individual agendas and discover what is best for the firm?

For a conversation like this, you need to start with questions that prompt creativity and force you to think strategically without getting bogged down with the details. This will be difficult; you are dealing with a business challenge wrapped in emotion. In order to keep focused on the big picture, you will need to continually refocus so your questions keep you from diving into the details.

What strategic questions *that don't drive an agenda* would you ask? Write them down.

FOR FURTHER CONSIDERATION

- *What do we want the result of this decision to be?*

- *Is one of us better at taking this business to the next level than the other?*

- *Is there a fair way to decide who gets to keep the firm and who gets the money?*

- *Does the firm need to stay as one business?*

- *Would it make sense if we split it and each took a part of it?*

Clearly these are wide-open questions. They are solely for the purpose of brainstorming about the future of the business. There are no right or wrong answers, just two people having a safe conversation about what to do with a successful business. You are not trying to solve anything at this point; you are trying to find options.

If you cannot get your partner and you to a place where you both are not afraid of losing something, this conversation cannot take place. When you drop your agenda there is a much greater chance of getting to a win-win situation.

Note: This is a true story. I was the consultant helping the two partners figure this out. When I asked, "Is one of you better at running a business than the other?" they both laughed because it was very clear that one of them was. They were able to move forward toward a sound financial agreement that bought out one partner and left the other running the company.

POSTSCRIPT

Suzie and I meet for ninety minutes every other week for the next year. She keeps her commitment of spending one day a week with one of her team members. Once she drops her agenda, she learns to ask a question, listen to the answer, and ask another one. In team meetings I hear her asking questions and getting input in a way she never had before. Now when she asks if everyone had a great weekend, her team is willing to share.

Her team blossoms and almost doubles its productivity in the next fiscal year. The Monday meetings take almost two hours now. There are lots of questions, lots of answers, and lots and lots of learning.

Suzie's first grandchild was born the next summer. She flew to San Francisco and stayed for a long weekend to help her daughter and to get to know her new granddaughter. She resumed playing competitive tennis and finally started using the mountain condo she bought five years ago. And she had foot surgery.

Cynthia left the office. She took a job with the company that supplies copiers to Suzie's office.

6

Check Your Motivation

Seth calls me on a Thursday morning.

"I'm thinking about moving one of our factory workers into a management position. He's been with us for almost 25 years and I think he may be ready to become our scheduler. I've been doing the scheduling for the past ten years and because of our growth, I can't keep up with both my work and scheduling. I'd like you to coach him through the process."

"What makes you think he needs coaching?"

"I am concerned about how the rest of the staff will react to this promotion. Mark is kind of quiet, but sometimes he can come across as a my-way-or-the-highway kind of guy. Truth is, he is very difficult to read. I'd appreciate your take on him. Why don't you meet and we can talk afterward."

I meet Mark a few days later at a coffee shop near the plant. Seth asked me to meet him offsite because no one else had been told about this potential promotion.

Mark is short for a man, about five and a half feet, very muscular, with a military style haircut. I start by asking Mark if he knows why we're meeting.

"Seth said it might help me make this transition."

"Are you concerned about the transition?"

"I don't know."

"Are you excited about this new position?"

"I think so."

"Are you concerned about your ability to be successful in this new position?"

Eight seconds of silence. And then, "No, not really."

"Mark, tell me about the work you've done here in the past. Tell me what you liked and what you did not like."

"I've worked in every department. I'm the best die maker this company has ever had. You can ask anyone, they'll tell you. Once they flew me to Hong Kong so I could help take apart a flexo machine and prepare it for shipping. When it was delivered here, I put it back together. I did it all by myself. I'd end up calling the guys in Hong Kong at three in the morning when I ran into a problem. That was pretty cool."

"Sounds pretty cool. What you do not like about working here?"

"Well, I don't like people problems. I hate it when two people can't get a job done because they disagree on how it should be done. They end up needing a mediator to solve their problems and it slows down the whole place. I just wish we could all do our work and forget the petty differences."

"What makes you think this scheduling position is the right spot for you?"

"I've been here for over 25 years. I guess they think it's time I worked in the office."

"Is that what you want?"

Mark shrugs his shoulders. "Sure."

"Mark, I have a problem with your 'Sure.' To me it sounds like a lack of commitment. If I ask my husband, 'Honey, do you love me?' and he says, 'Sure,' it would not feel as good as a resounding 'Yes.'"

Mark laughs. I press on.

"Mark, I've never worked as a scheduler in your industry, but I am guessing that there are going to be a lot of strong sales personalities who are going to want their jobs to have priority on the production schedule. So far, in our very brief time together, what I've seen from you is a mix of indecision, no decision, and very slow decision. Do you see what I see?"

"But I'm not going to be running the daily scheduling meeting right away. Seth is going to continue to run them until I am comfortable in the new position."

"Do you think you will learn how to best run a scheduling meeting by watching Seth?"

Eight seconds of silence. Shoulder shrug. "It can't hurt."

. . .

Seth is an excellent leader. He's well read and always willing to try new ideas. We have known each other for fifteen years, but I can't figure out what he is thinking with regard to making Mark the scheduler. It does not seem like a good fit.

I phone Seth and ask to see him the next day.

When we meet, I get right to the point. "Seth, help me here. What is your rationale for putting Mark in the scheduling position?"

"He has been with us for over 25 years. His father worked here until a few years ago. He is the best die maker we have ever had, and a very loyal employee. I am concerned that if

I don't give him this promotion, we will lose him, and I do not want to lose him. This seems like a position that he could handle."

"A position he could handle?"

"He could grow into it given the right amount of time."

"How much time?"

"I don't know. I guess that depends on Mark."

"Seth, who are you serving by putting Mark in this position?"

"Mark. I'm giving him an opportunity to grow with the company."

I'm beginning to see the problem.

"Seth, you and I have spent a lot of time talking about asking questions in order to develop those around you. However, I forgot one piece. In order to develop yourself, you have to be able to ask yourself questions, too. It's called checking your motivation."

Seth scratches his head. "What do you mean?"

"If you ask yourself what it is about Mark that makes you believe he would be a good scheduler, what would your answer be?"

"I'd say something like, 'He'll be okay. I will give him loads of support. I will run the daily scheduling meeting until Mark is ready to take over.'"

"That's not answering the question. What is it about Mark *right now* that makes you think he will be a success as the scheduling manager?"

Seth just stares at me. I can tell he is really struggling with this. I take a different tack.

"Seth, what makes you good at running a scheduling meeting?"

"I know the salespeople. I know their hot buttons and I know what matters to them. I also know the customers, and that helps tremendously when trying to make scheduling decisions. I guess my institutional knowledge is a key factor here."

"Did you ask yourself if Mark's institutional knowledge is the same as yours?"

"Mark knows every nook and cranny on the factory floor. He can fix any machine that breaks. He knows the maintenance schedule better than our maintenance guy! He stays late when we need him and comes in on weekends when necessary."

"That's not what I'm asking. Do you and Mark have the same type of institutional knowledge?"

Seth laughs. "I can't fix one darn machine on the factory floor. I wouldn't know a maintenance procedure if my life depended on it."

Now it's my turn to laugh. "Seth, how well does Mark know his fellow employees?"

"I have no idea. He doesn't really interact with a lot of folks here. He pretty much keeps to himself."

"So, if I understand you correctly, you are planning on putting your most technically competent employee, who is somewhat indecisive and does not interact a lot with the other employees, into a position that demands no technical skills but does demand a high level of interaction with others and quick decision-making ability. Is that correct, or am I missing something?"

Seth covers his eyes with his hand and moans.

"What am I going to do? I don't want to lose him. I already told him about this office position. I don't think I can go back on my word."

"It appears to me that you have two choices. What are they?"

Seth sighs.

"Let Mark take the job and see if he can do it, or tell him I made a mistake and that scheduling is not the right fit for him."

He brightens. "Or maybe there's a third choice. Maybe I could find him another spot in the front office."

"Which choice makes the most sense?"

"If I give Mark the scheduling position and he fails, then he has to go back to the printing floor. That would be extremely embarrassing for him. He has always been successful here. He might leave us just to save face.

"If I give him the scheduling job and he turns out to be great at it, that would be great. And it would also be a miracle.

"Or I could look around for another job for him."

"What would your motivation be for finding him another job? Taking care of Mark, or taking care of yourself?"

His shoulders slump. "If I tell him I've decided he is not the right guy for the job, then I have to explain to him why not, and that would be so unkind."

"What's more unkind: putting him in a position where he will most likely fail, or explaining the mistake *you* made?"

"Right now they both feel terrible."

"What about sharing the whole story with him? Tell him that you offered him this position because you were afraid if you didn't give him the opportunity to move into management, he'd leave. Can you tell him that?"

"I can." He gets a devilish grin on his face. "But doesn't it have to be in the form of a question?"

He's got it! "Great idea!" I reply. "How could you pose that in a question?"

"I'd ask him if he knew why I offered him a management position. And then I'd explain myself further. It would definitely engage him."

"Why did you choose to keep this idea so close to the vest, Seth? Right now the only people who know you've put out feelers to Mark are the two of you and me."

Seth laughs.

"I guess I was hoping for some validation from you that would make me feel more secure in this decision."

"Sorry about that, Seth. What have you got to lose by telling Mark the truth and working through his reaction?"

"I guess nothing except the fact that this will be a very, very uncomfortable conversation."

"Seth, where do you grow the most: during uncomfortable conversations or comfortable conversations?"

"I know, I know. It's the uncomfortable ones. I have to engage Mark and ask him lots of questions."

"Can you look at this uncomfortable conversation as an opportunity for growth?"

"Maybe after I am done being sick to my stomach," Seth says grimly.

· · ·

Shortly after Seth and I work on the questions to ask and Mark's possible responses, he has his talk with Mark. As predicted, it is not an easy conversation. Seth asks lots of questions and Mark gives him very little feedback. He nods as Seth explains what his motivations were. He nods as Seth asks if Mark understands that Seth was afraid of losing a great employee.

"Is this a huge disappointment for you?" Seth asks Mark.

"Kind of."

"Kind of in what way?"

"I liked the idea of having an office, and I liked the idea of being in the front of the building as opposed to the back. But every once in a while, I thought I might miss working on the floor with the machinery."

Then Seth comes up with a question that changes the entire conversation.

"Mark, are you happy working here?" Seth asks.

"Most days, yeah. It's always challenging when personalities get in the way of getting our work done, but I guess that's just life. I'm not sure I'd still be here after 25 years if I didn't like it."

"Is there anything I can do to increase your job satisfaction, short of a raise, that is?"

"Do you think I could attend some of those management team meetings you have? The ones where you all get together and talk about the future of the company? I think I might have some good ideas for this place."

Seth smiles. "I'd have to bring that to the management team and get their thoughts. Off the top of my head, I think there may be a good fit there. Give me some time to do my homework and let's talk again."

"Sure," Mark answers.

. . .

When Seth shares the results of his conversation with me, we are both quite pleased—Seth because he has a happy ending, me because I see that Seth is growing in his ability to develop those around him by asking the right questions.

"What did you learn from this?" I ask Seth.

"I almost blew it, that's what I learned."

We both laugh, but I persist. "Why? What did you miss?"

"Somehow I got this idea in my head that it was time for Mark to join management and that he'd leave if I didn't find him a spot. So I came up with a job for him and offered it to him. What was I thinking?"

"You were actually thinking a lot. What were you *not* doing?"

"I wasn't asking questions."

"Why not?"

"I'm not sure. It just seemed like I was operating inside my own head and everything was making sense at the time."

"What question will you use in the future?"

"I will ask myself what my motivation is. I don't ever want to go through this again."

What Type of Question Helps You Check Your Own Motivations?

Gus and Don have worked together for over 16 years. They are good friends and socialize outside of the workplace. Initially, they were peers, most recently as quality directors, but three years ago Gus was promoted to VP of Quality, becoming Don's boss. There are seven quality directors working for Gus, including Terri.

Gus has been asked to prepare a succession plan. He's having a hard time making a decision between Terri and Don; they both have important qualities that would serve the quality team.

Last week his team spent two days at an offsite retreat planning the future of their Six Sigma group and discussing supplier quality and the quality in the plants. During that offsite meeting, it became more clear to Gus that Terri too, has strong leadership skills and is able to see outside her box to the bigger picture. Gus notes with some dismay that she's ahead of Don in this area.

When I speak with Gus, he's conflicted. He'll be leaving his position in eighteen months as part of a routine rotation. He needs to get his successor into executive coaching so he or she will be ready to move into the position when the time comes.

His choices are:

- Have Terri coached and tell Don he is not getting the job

- Have Don coached and hope that he can develop the necessary skills

- Have them both coached and promote whoever comes out learning more

Checking the motivations of others usually is not difficult. Being able to check your own motivations can be downright impossible, because often you're emotionally invested in the outcome. You want things to go your way.

If you were Gus, what questions would you ask yourself in order to check your own motivation? Take out a piece of paper and write them down.

FOR FURTHER CONSIDERATION

Some of the questions I'd ask in the Gus/Don/Terri situation would be:

- *Who will benefit from this decision?*

- *Who could be hurt by this decision?*

- *If Don doesn't get this job, will I be disappointed? If yes, why will I be disappointed?*

- *Is there another way to do this?*

- *How much input have I asked for with regard to this decision?*

- *Have I considered all potential sources of information?*

- *Do I really already know who the best candidate is?*

- *On what am I basing my decision?*

POSTSCRIPT

Seth brings the idea of including Mark in management team meetings to the management team and the response is resoundingly positive. In fact, the overall sense from the team is, "Why didn't we think of this sooner? Mark is an integral part of caring for one of our greatest capital investments: our machinery. His input is key to many of the decisions we make."

Mark now attends quarterly management team meetings. Sometimes he just listens instead of talking, but he is present and available.

Seth and Mark's relationship has changed, too. Now they talk about whether the production floor is designed for the highest level of productivity, if the company is ready to purchase another flexo machine, if deeper dock wells would allow them to use larger transport vehicles and serve their customers more efficiently.

Mark still works at the printing company. Seth has delegated his human resource-related tasks, such as compensation and benefits, to a new staff member, and his training responsibilities to the quality leader, but he still runs the scheduling meeting every morning.

7

Don't Be So Sure You're Sure

I am asked to coach Trish and Sally, who have just been invited to join the Partner Development Program at a regional architectural firm.

The Partner Development Program is a two-year process for individuals the firm considers to have the greatest potential as partners. The individuals in the program function as closely as possible as partners, although without the financial ramifications. They attend all partner meetings, both social- and work-related. They are privy to personnel decisions, financial decisions, and any other major decisions made by the partner group, on the theory that "to become, you must act as if you already are." Partnership Development is an excellent way for both potential and existing partners to get a feel for who the future partners will be.

As is my practice, I meet with both potential coachees before I commit, because it's important that the chemistry be right.

· · ·

I meet Trish first. She's overweight and disheveled; her clothes don't seem to fit her quite right. Her eyeglasses are too tight for her face; when she takes them off to wipe her brow, which she does frequently, they leave their imprint on her temples. She carries a soda bottle and plays with it while she talks. She's jittery, perhaps because of her caffeinated soda intake. She talks fast but in circles, giving me much more information than I need, frequently saying "Don't tell anybody, but…"

Her extended family is blue collar. Her father works in a factory, but recently lost his job. Her mother works at a grocery store now; formerly she was a waitress. She has two brothers, neither of whom has a college degree: one delivers packages for FedEx; the other is a bartender. She has good relationships with all her family members but feels a strain because she is in a more professional occupation than any of the others.

We spend two hours together. It seems much longer.

Then I meet Sally, who is well dressed and fit, not a hair out of place. Her buttoned-down blue shirt works well with her strawberry blond hair. Sally speaks slowly and seems to choose her words carefully. She talks about her husband, the recent birth of their fourth child, and the three boys they already have. When I ask a question, she answered it succinctly and knows how to completely finish a thought, but her answers seem almost guarded.

Her extended family consists of her dad, who is an engineering professor at a large university, her mom, who is a homemaker, and her brother, who is an engineer with a Fortune 500 company. They all live within thirty miles of each other and spend holidays together.

We spend one hour together.

I decide there is enough chemistry in both relationships to move forward. After three coaching sessions, I meet with the managing partner and the partner to whom both these women report.

My feedback is this: Sally will be the easier of the two to get to partner. She needs to get a better understanding of how to build relationships, she needs to make a personal commitment to coaching, she needs to open up more so that she can learn to develop her staff and put them at ease around her.

Trish is another story. She has as many fingers in as many pies as she can. She places blame on others. She is a busybody, with too many "Don't tell anyone this, but…" relationships at any given time. I'll need to help her slow down and think, and I am not sure Trish will be able to reflect at the level she needs to in order to be successful.

The two partners seem surprised at this assessment, which surprises me.

We decide to meet again in two months, when Trish and Sally will each have experienced seven coaching sessions.

. . .

In those next two months, both women begin to unfold.

Sally goes through the motions of meeting with me, but doesn't really try to alter her behavior. She thinks she's building relationships, but her staff sees no change. When one of the partners asks her how the coaching is going, she responds that she isn't getting much out of it. She also does not do her homework assignments. She is not moving forward.

Trish, on the other hand, digs in enthusiastically. She slows down. She reflects on her actions and motivations. She slowly backs away from unnecessary involvements, focusing only on what she needs to be involved in. She no longer says, "Don't tell anyone, but…"

I tell her to leave the soda bottle on her desk, and she does. She struggles with leaving behind the Nosy Nellie persona, but she finally sees how freeing it is. As we continue our work, she slowly changes herself in the workplace. In fact, it appears that she also changes her relationship with her husband and the way she parents her children. She stops telling, she starts asking.

She gets it.

So, two months later, I return to the two partners with my tail between my legs.

"I was wrong about Trish and Sally," I tell them.

They both smile, first at me and then at each other. I nod and smile also. We almost don't need to say anything else. I was only saying what they'd known all along.

Trish is coachable…very coachable, in fact. She just needs an objective outsider to ask the difficult questions that make her squirm, but also make her think. Trish is working at a pace that will take her to the partnership level.

Sally is a different story. She does not "get it." She is not open to the coaching experience. What looked promising on the outside is not what it appears. Sally has answers to my questions, but they're all on the surface. She has no interest in digging any deeper. Sally might need a life-changing event to make her see how she needs to change in order to be partner material.

What a learning experience for me! I had fallen into the trap of judging a book by its cover. Fortunately, the coachability assessment I conducted was set up so that it worked despite my initial impression! I can't emphasize enough that once you commit to help develop the potential in others, success depends on your ability to be open-minded. Unless you ask questions to learn what is happening in another's reality, you cannot be sure you are sure.

Here's the experience that really taught me this concept: I was coaching Kayla, an executive who had 18 direct reports. When I started her assessment, I realized that it would be unfair to leave anyone out of the loop, so I spoke with all 18 people. When I do an assessment, I am always looking for common threads, and the one that stood out in Kayla's was that people consistently commented that she was never in a good mood. She never laughed with her team.

At our next meeting I observed her body language. I couldn't believe what I saw. I had to ask her about it.

"Do you know that you never smile?" I asked her.

"I don't?"

"No, I have never seen you with a big grin on your face."

She looked down at her pad of paper. It was very quiet.

"It's from my childhood," she said. "I have never liked my dimples. I started hating them when I was in kindergarten. I used to dream I could have them removed by surgery when I got old enough. I practiced in front of a mirror so I could smile just enough to not have my dimples show. I thought it was enough of a smile. No one has ever mentioned that I don't smile."

She looked at me with tears in her eyes.

"It really affects how people react to you," I said. "Almost every member of your team mentioned that you are never in a good mood, that you don't laugh even when something really funny happens."

"I never knew anyone noticed."

"How do you feel about your dimples now?" I asked.

"I never even think of them. I've been not smiling for so long that it has become my natural way of being. I could care less about them now."

"Do you think you could try smiling a little bigger? Let people see when you are happy? I'm no shrink, but there is some truth to the old saying *Smile and the world smiles with you, cry and you cry alone.* I also know I have a hard time thinking negative thoughts when I have a smile on my face."

She agreed to make a conscious effort to smile more.

We met again one month later. When I asked how the smiling was going, she laughed.

"What's so funny?" I asked.

"You're going to think I'm a freak."

"All my clients are freaks," I assured her.

"Since I've been trying to smile—and I don't even know if I do or if anyone has noticed—the weird thing is, I just feel so much happier. I am in a better mood all the time. I mean all the time. Life seems like so much more fun. It's amazing."

Don't be so sure you are sure. The person I thought was an ornery client was just someone who needed to learn how to smile.

THE CHALLENGE
How to Be Sure You're Sure

Are you more often sure about a situation, or unsure? Either way, you need to get in touch with your underlying thoughts so you avoid saying one thing when you actually think or feel another.

What questions could you ask yourself when you are quite sure that you're sure about something?

How can you double-check your thought processes so you don't do what I did, and judge the book by its cover?

Is there a particular situation in your company where this might be happening right now?

What questions can you ask yourself that go deeper, questions that would help you be sure you are sure? Write down the particular situation you are dealing with, and then write down questions that will force you to reconsider just how sure you are.

FOR FURTHER CONSIDERATION

In an effort to not be sure you are so sure, it helps tremendously if you can engage others who are not tied to the event to help you find an objective voice.

Questions you might ask them include:

- *I've explained the situation to you. Are there any blind spots you see that I don't?*

- *If you were me, is there anything you would do differently?*

- *Have you ever had a situation like this? Can you tell me about it?*

Remember, the key here is to listen to the answers, not to get defensive. Don't bother asking if you are unable to listen!

POSTSCRIPT

Trish becomes a partner eighteen months after we start our work together.

Sally leaves the firm and takes a job with the Army Corps of Engineers.

Both are happy.

8

Take Ownership of Your Challenges by Asking Questions

Brenda has been in her new position with a large semi-conductor company for eighteen months. The promotion has taken her, and her family, from a laid-back regional office in Los Angeles to the corporate headquarters in St. Louis. Her family has adjusted well to the very different culture of an old and comparatively traditional city, and is thriving. Actually, the family is doing better than Brenda.

Brenda does not thrive in the corporate culture of the home office. The success she achieved in a regional office, where she led her own team and had greater control over her results, does not translate well to the home office and its bureaucracy. Brenda is, in effect, an extremely successful entrepreneur who had been promoted for just that reason. And the same thing happens to her as happens to many great salespeople who are promoted to sales manager. A great salesperson knows how to close a deal, but not necessarily how to manage other people on a day-to-day basis.

Some of these promotees realize this early on and happily move back into the sales force, where they are more successful and probably make more money. Some of these individuals decide to make a go of it and try to learn the skills it takes to manage people. Some of them are successful, some of them are not.

Brenda decides to give it a try. I am asked to coach her.

Brenda is a very likeable person. She tells funny stories in which she is often the butt of the joke. She is able to laugh at herself and has a high energy level. It's energizing just to be around her. She is a get-it-done kind of person—give her a challenge and she'll tackle it like a linebacker.

And Brenda has her downside.

· · ·

Like so many of the people I have coached, Brenda is a talker. In the course of two 90-minute meetings, I realize I have to go head-to-head with her. During the course of our work together, I tell her she is a name-dropper, I tell her she is a show-off and I tell her she really isn't as good as she thinks she is. There are several times she could have thrown me out of her office. She doesn't.

Brenda says she is sick and tired of "corporate bullshit." She appears to be at the end of her rope. My first question is, "Do you want to try to weed through this, or is it time to find another job?"

Brenda decides to rise to the challenge.

"I have to learn to deal with this stuff," she said. "It would probably show up at my next job, anyway. I have to learn to work with a bureaucracy. The trouble is, I have no idea where to start."

We continue our work together.

"What is it that bugs you so much about the corporate setting?" I ask.

"So many meetings, so many reports, so many people who move at a snail's pace. I want my guys to sell stuff. I want to get things done. I can't do that if I have to get signatures every time one of my team passes gas. They want to make my guys start filling out time logs so they can tell exactly where the people in the field are spending their time—in 15-minute increments. They actually want them to put it in a spreadsheet so they can analyze it. This is never going to fly—these are sales guys!"

I begin to understand Brenda's struggles. She isn't asking questions, she isn't getting to the "why."

Brenda needs to ask questions to help her better understand what needs to be done.

She isn't taking ownership of what needs to be done. She is being the victim.

And most importantly, she isn't asking questions that will help her help her team members take ownership and achieve the results they want.

"Why do you think you know how this place should be run?"

"Maybe I don't. You just told me I'm not as good as I think I am. But if they want us to sell stuff, they should leave us alone so we can go sell it."

"That sounds like the sales guys want to operate independently of the organization. Does that make sense to you?"

"No, and I realize that…intellectually. But I can't seem to get past my frustration with the organization as a whole."

"Is there any chance that's because you are not taking ownership?"

"What do you mean by that?"

"Is there any chance you are not taking ownership here?

"Ownership of what?"

"Of the importance of working together with the rest of the leadership team? How much poison are you pouring into your team, into the people around you, the entire organization?"

"Poison?"

"Do you tell your team that you know it's a hassle, but the firm really needs the information on those time sheets to confirm that your resources are all in the right place? Or do you tell them it's just another corporate initiative and you hate it as much as they do?"

"The second part." Brenda is nothing if not honest.

"And how do you react to the people who asked you for the information?"

"I told them it's crap and a waste of time."

"Making friend all over the place, aren't you?"

"But it *is* crap!"

"Regardless, Brenda, you need to take ownership and find a way to make this work. You tell me you want to. Are you ready?"

"Yes."

. . .

Brenda and I work together once every three weeks. After three months, here's what we discover.

Brenda is a "teller" of the highest degree. In order to move her style to one of developing her team by asking questions, we have to take drastic measures. Her first assignment is to never make a declarative statement when one of her people calls her with a challenge. She is only allowed to make an interrogative statement. And she does it!

A few weeks later, before our next scheduled meeting, I am facilitating a sales training for the same firm. I have never met any of the thirty participants before. At the first break, a woman approaches me and says, "Maureen, I am so happy to meet you. I have heard so much about you through Brenda. Can I tell you a funny story?"

I immediately guide this woman to a quiet corner. She tells me Brenda had come to Charlotte the week after our second coaching meeting.

"I had a major challenge on my plate," she tells me, "and when we sat down to discuss it, Brenda started asking one question after another. Finally I asked her to stop with the questions and just tell me what to do! But she said she wasn't allowed to!

"She told me, 'I have this executive coach named Maureen who told me I can't tell anyone anything; I have to help them find the answers by asking them questions.'

"Long story short: I figured out what I needed to do, even thought it was painful. The funny thing is, now I find myself doing the same thing with my people. I ask them what they think they should do."

She tells me her entire office has a new feel to it.

"People are thinking harder and considering many more options than ever before. I really think this is going to help our sales model, that we are going to open more doors than ever before because we are all working differently."

Way to go, Brenda! But she still has the time-log challenge to deal with.

· · ·

"Do you understand why they have asked you to do this?" I ask during our next coaching session.

"They want to assess our resources."

"Do you think this is the best way to assess your resources?"

"I think there has to be a better way."

"Have you asked if anyone has a better idea?"

"Who would I ask?"

"Who do you think you might ask?" (See how this works? Just because someone asks you a question doesn't mean you have to answer it!)

"I could ask my boss. I could ask his boss. Or I could ask my guys in the field."

"Is there any reason you would not ask them all?"

· · ·

The next time I walk into a meeting with Brenda, she is smiling from ear to ear.

"This is going to be good," I say. "Forget the questions—tell me what's happening!"

"I went to ask my boss if it was okay if I talked with *his* boss, Jillian, about the time charting," Brenda reports. "He wasn't thrilled about the idea, but I asked him to trust me and promised that I would not be belligerent or make a scene of any sort. He gave me the okay, and when I talked with Jillian, I had all sort of questions ready. I wrote them down just like you and I discussed. I asked her to share the history of the project with me, and what the hope was for the results.

"It turns out the CEO was behind this; he'd asked Jillian if she knew where her sales engineers were spending their time. Jillian didn't have an answer, and that worried her. She decided it was probably a good idea to have the sales reps all log their time so she could gather that information and report back to the CEO. Right away, I could sense from her tone of voice how it must have felt to not have the answer when her boss asked her.

"I asked her if I could help. She laughed somewhat dismissively, but I decide to move forward and asked if she thought requiring the entire sales force to log their time was a good idea. She said it seemed like the best one to her.

"So I asked her if she thought she was going to get good empirical data. She said she wasn't sure but that she had no other ideas and that she *had* to have this information.

"I asked her if she'd be interested in me finding out if the guys out in the trenches had any ideas on how best to quantify where they spend their time. She told me that was fine, but that she was short on time so I'd better get on it quick.

"So before I called the sales guys, I called an actuary I knew from grad school. I didn't have the skills to figure this out, but I thought he might. He told me we would not have to make every single sales rep keep a time log; all we needed was a slice of the population that we could really depend on to give us the best information. He suggested we add a bonus for those willing to help out. That way we would have the best data possible and a much, much happier sales force. It seemed like a win-win to me.

"I called my sales managers and we discussed the idea. I asked them if they knew why we were doing this data collection. Not one of them knew. When I asked them questions that helped them get to the "why" I could hear the relief in their voices, even through the phone lines. I had the questions written down in front of me, it came together like clockwork. Suddenly it all made sense to everyone.

"Then I asked if they thought they could find three sales engineers in their district willing to help us with this project. Without hesitation, each sales manager said yes. I asked if they thought the bonus would help…and the amazing part is, they didn't think we'd need it. Each sales manager believed that if they shared the reasoning behind the project, they would find willing participants.

"I brought my idea back to Jillian, along with some support data from my actuary buddy. Jillian thought it was great. She didn't even think we needed to go to the CEO with our process; she was so confident that this would work.

"We've identified the project participants. We've designed the data-entry process. And Jillian has been able to tell our CEO that she will have a report on his desk on 90 days."

All this from asking a few questions! Brenda has clearly learned to take ownership of herself. She digs in deeper than any client I have ever experienced.

As we continue our work together, Brenda takes the art of asking questions to a new level. Not only did she learn the art of asking questions on her own, she begins to demand it from her staff as well. I start hearing them say things like this:

"No one has ever poured themselves into me the way Brenda has."

"I have never had this much development time with my boss, ever."

"Brenda is teaching me things that I will take with me wherever my career leads. I am so fortunate to work with her."

Brenda is my poster child. Never has a client worked this hard to understand the power of developing themselves and the people around them by asking questions.

THE CHALLENGE
Take Ownership

Are there areas in your work where you are not taking ownership?

Is there a part of your job that feels out of control?

Is there a situation in which you think you have no options?

Are you allowing yourself to be the victim?

Name it by writing it down. Now think about how you can take ownership of this area, this part of your job, or this situation. Think about it—who else could you discuss this with? What questions do you need to ask to take ownership of this challenge?

FOR FURTHER CONSIDERATION

One of the best ways to recognize when you are not taking ownership is by using the whining meter. If there is something happening in your organization that is driving you nuts and you find yourself giving it excessive emotional energy, aka you are whining about it, you need to check whether you are taking ownership or not. Questions you can ask yourself are:

- *Why does this bother me so much?*

- *What have I done to face this challenge?*

- *Am I promoting poison?*

- *How can I promote a solution?*

- *Am I being petty?*

- *Do my actions affect my team?*

This is a good challenge to discuss with someone who is completely independent of the situation, someone who does not work with you and has nothing to do with your industry.

POSTSCRIPT

Brenda is still working in the St. Louis corporate office. She is in a much better place than when we started. She continues to believe that asking questions is the greatest thing she can do to develop the people around you. She is a master of taking ownership of her challenges and resolving them by asking questions and gathering information.

When I go on tour with this book, I want to take her with me.

9

Ask Questions Even When
You Know the Answers

"I don't need you anymore! I totally get this question stuff!"
Jerome says as I enter his office for our third executive
coaching session.

"That's great!" I shoot back at him. "But just in case, let's
talk a bit more."

· · ·

I knew Jerome was doing well. His boss had called me to say
that he could not believe the results we had achieved after just
two coaching sessions. He told me that Jerome was engaged in
the conversation and was asking questions. He'd even stopped
himself at one point and said, "Now my coach would tell me
to ask a question here…"

Initially, I'd been thrilled with Jerome's ability to dive in
head first, wanting to "get it" as quickly as possible. Jerome is
a very quick study. That's what got him this far.

It is also the reason I am asked to coach him.

· · ·

Jerome started as a "sales guy" who quickly moved to sales manager. His leadership skills are apparent to those around him, and when the opportunity to run one of the business units opened up, he was the number one candidate for the job. Shortly after that, the vice president of sales position opened up, and Jerome was chosen for that promotion. Jerome is vice president of sales for a $1 billion privately held consumer products corporation. He is successful in his work and well liked. His team knows what he expects of them and what they can expect from him.

What got Jerome to this spot were tenacity, intellect, charm and desire. What might cause him to fail is his inability to listen to others because he has decided that he already knows the answers. He knows the right path to take to achieve a goal and the right way to deal with a challenge at hand.

This wasn't such a big deal when he was a sales manager, or even when he ran a business unit. Ninety percent of the time, Jerome was correct! But back then, the decisions were smaller, and so were the consequences. Now Jerome has peers who are a talented group of people and who are accustomed to being heard and having all angles considered. The approach that had worked for Jerome throughout his entire professional career is no longer working. Can he adjust?

After our second meeting, Jerome takes our work to heart. He lets his team know he's being coached. He lets his peers know he is being coached. In fact, he tells anyone who will listen that he's being coached.

He explains to each of them that he is trying to ask more questions in order to learn to be a better listener. This is what prompted his boss to call me to marvel about the results we'd achieved after just two coaching sessions!

So why was I concerned?

Jerome loves a challenge. When you give him one, you'd better step out of the way because he's already starting to work on it, the sooner the better. After a ninety-minute conversation, "asking questions" becomes Jerome's mantra for the next few weeks. He's determined to get it right.

Sustainability is a key ingredient in developing your people. The effort has to be constant. Jerome is trying to check the box, to get this question-asking skill mastered as quickly as possible so he can move on to the next challenge. He has an assignment; he does what he has to to get it done.

Unfortunately for Jerome, there is no way he is going to internalize this skill with just two weeks of practice. Learning to listen is a life-altering practice, and he needs to dig much deeper to make this skill part of who he is rather than just something he does.

More importantly, I am not seeing the question-asking side of Jerome during our coaching meetings. He's still on overdrive. He does not ask me questions, and he interrupts constantly. When I leave after our third coaching session, I see a friend in the hallway near Jerome's office. We do the usual hello-how-are-you greeting and I hear myself say, "I am exhausted!"

I wonder how many of the people Jerome interacts with on a daily basis feel the same way. In person, communicating with Jerome is exhausting. If I worked with him on a daily basis, I would communicate via email at every opportunity.

I decide to go back to the six people I interviewed for my preliminary 360 when I was evaluating Jerome for coachability. I want their take on whether Jerome is changing.

I start with his peers and direct reports. What I learn is that Jerome is asking a lot of questions, but he generally interrupts others in order to ask them (and then he blames me for it by continually mentioning that his coach told him to ask lots of questions!).

Here's what his peers and direct reports say:

- Before I can finish my thought, Jerome throws another question at me. It feels like a filibuster. He's just trying to keep it going and going.

- It doesn't feel as if Jerome takes my input seriously. He has always been data-driven but now he's taking it to an extreme. We can't even have a people conversation anymore. It's all about what the data says.

- It feels like we are in a fire drill most of the time we are together!

But his boss has a very different perception.

- Jerome brings some good strategic thinking to the table. He considers many angles and asks excellent questions that help us drill down to what really matters. He seems more engaged in our conversations.

What I soon realize is that Jerome asks very good questions when he is "managing up," but potentially useless questions when he's with his peers or his team.

Slowing Jerome down to look at why he interrupts people is one of the greatest challenges I have encountered. As we move along in our coaching relationship, there are times when I actually have to stand up and say firmly, "Do not interrupt me!"

He tells me once, "Oh, I don't do that when I am with other people. I just do it with you."

"Not good enough! You need to not-interrupt *all* the time." I take a deep breath, because I am going to have to ask hard questions, and I wanted my voice as neutral as possible.

"Jerome, have you ever noticed that you are more apt to break into conversations that your peers or your team members are having with each other than you are with senior management?

"And have you ever noticed that you overwhelm your peers and direct reports with a barrage of sometimes useless or hostile questions, but when you're with senior management, you slow down, pay attention to what people say, and ask great questions?"

Jerome thinks for a few moments.

"Honestly? I know I am smarter than my peers, and I know I am smarter than my team. I want them to get it faster. I feel as if I am pulling them all the time. But when I am with senior management, I have to slow down because I know I don't know everything they know. I will someday, but not just yet."

"Jerome, how are you using the art of asking questions when you are with senior management?"

"I learn so much when I am with them. I get to ask questions that, to be quite honest, I always wanted the answers to! I find myself really learning and getting a better understanding of the business and where they want it to go."

"Okay, now tell me how you are using the art of asking questions when you work with your peers or your team?"

"I use it to help them get to the point faster, to cut to the chase."

"Jerome, what would happen if you tried to use your senior management questioning style when you worked with your peers and your team?"

"Our meetings would take forever. They don't always have the answers to my questions. Senior management always seems to have the answers."

"Are you asking questions only to get an answer?"

"Why else would I ask a question?"

I realize with a sinking heart that Jerome hasn't absorbed one very important piece of the process: *In order to develop your people, you ask questions, not because **you** necessarily need the answer, but because **they** need the answer.*

Jerome is too tied up in work to see the problem, so I use a non-work example.

"Jerome, when your son or daughter comes home an hour later than curfew without calling, and you've been pacing the kitchen floor worried to death, what questions do you want to ask them?"

"Where have you been? Why didn't you call?"

"Is that really what you want to know?"

"No! I want them to know how sick to my stomach I've been for the past hour! I want them to know that I have to go to work the next day and perform at one hundred percent even though they robbed me of a good night's sleep! I want them to know that they've taken a few years off my life due to the stress they just put me through!"

"Exactly. Now tell me how would you pose those questions."

"What do you think my world was like for the past hour? What time do I go to work in the morning? How much sleep do you think I'll get tonight? What's on my schedule tomorrow that really, really matters? If you took my blood pressure right now, do you know how high it would be?"

"What, in essence, are you getting at with this son or daughter?"

"I am trying to get them to walk a mile in my shoes."

"So when you are at work, can you help others see things that you already know instead of being impatient with your staff and your peers?"

"I've always been a bit impatient. The difference is that I used to just tell them what to do. Now you tell me I have to ask them questions, so I am and it's driving me nuts. Half the time they don't have an answer!"

"Is it possible that you are asking the wrong questions, that your focus is not on helping them develop their skills but rather on getting information so you can move along? Is it possible that your questions are serving *you* rather than developing *them*?"

Jerome looks stunned.

The art of asking questions in order to develop others sometimes includes asking questions to which you already know the answer.

It's important to not confuse this with being condescending.

"When that son or daughter came home an hour late," I tell Jerome, "your questions were a way of telling them what you just went through. Where they were and why they didn't call really don't matter once they're home safely. Your hope is that the next time they're going to be late, they'll think to call and let you know. Your questions were, in essence, developing your son or daughter."

I ask Jerome to think about this for a while, and we'll revisit the issue in a week.

· · ·

Our next meeting does not start out like the previous one. Jerome does not tell me, "I don't need you anymore!"

Instead, he greets me with, "This is hard work. I have to think all the time. It's like my brain has to work twice as hard. One side of my brain is engaged in the conversation, the other side is thinking, 'How can I help them see what really matters here?' It's exhausting."

Jerome is starting to get it. We have a lot more work to do, but he now understands that in order to develop your people, you must ask questions, and those questions are not to serve you, they are to serve them.

And you don't only ask questions to which you need an answer. You ask questions to help others learn.

THE CHALLENGE
Ask Questions Even When You Know the Answers

When you already know the answer, it is infinitely more difficult to ask a question. All your instincts scream, "You know the answer, so just tell them!" In some ways, that is what makes this chapter the most important—and the most difficult.

If you have been in a leadership position for more than one year, you probably have given reviews to some of your staff. And you probably know that there should be no surprises when it comes to reviews. If you've been doing your job, you've been talking with your people on a regular basis.

What you may not know is that reviews need to be done with interrogative statements, not declarative statements. You do not tell people about their work performance; rather, you ask them what they think of their work performance. Why? Because they will not hear you if you tell them. You must engage them, and you can only engage them by asking them how *they* think they are performing, not by you telling them how they are performing.

The result of doing this is a tremendous increase in ownership; you will have a much more accountable employee. What would you rather experience: having a boss tell you how you are performing, or telling your boss how you think you are performing? The latter makes most people squirm in their seats! Most people would rather sit quietly and let the words wash over them while their thoughts are either *Yeah, that's right, that's me* or *Is this guy crazy, I am so much better than that!* Either way, you have not engaged the employee.

Think of one of your direct reports. Now think of the questions you would use to be effective in their review.

What questions would you ask that person to help them understand how you perceived their review? Write them down.

FOR FURTHER CONSIDERATION

The review process is really very simple. I don't understand why so many companies make them so formal and time consuming. These are the questions I would ask:

- *What three things did you do really well?*

- *What three things do you need to work on?*

- *What would you like me to do differently?*

- *What would you like the company to do differently?*

Once you have that information, the employee can write his or her own action plan. In addition, you have obtained great feedback about your own abilities and for the company. I promise you, if you do this every year, not only will you get better at it, but your employees will get better at it too.

And if next year you see the same thing on the list of what someone needs to work on, what have you learned? And if you hear the same thing that your people want you to do differently, what have you learned? The results are powerful.

The first two questions on the list are questions to which you already know the answer. Just because you know doesn't mean you need to tell. Ask!

The result will serve you more than you can imagine.

POSTSCRIPT

Jerome takes our work to heart. He consumes himself in learning the art of asking questions that help develop others. Today he is sought out when a challenge arises. His people and his peers know he will help them leave no stone unturned.

Jerome recently learns that he is one of three people listed on the succession plan for the next CEO. He calls me to tell me, and I can't help but ask him, "Do you want it?"

"Funny you should ask. I was just asking myself the same question. See, I've even learned to develop myself by asking myself questions! I always thought it was I wanted, but now I am not so sure."

"What's changed?"

"I've had a chance to watch what happens when someone becomes CEO. They have no time for their family. Their health frequently deteriorates. They have no peers. It is lonely at the top and I am not sure I want to be there.

"I really like my work right now," he goes on. "I have a great work-life balance, I have time to take care of me, and I am fulfilled by my work. I am just not sure at this point. I'm going to keep asking myself questions until I get an answer that feels right for me and for my family."

Jerome is still on the succession plan. He still doesn't know what he will do if chosen. My hope is that he'll ask a few questions.

10

Sustain, Maintain, and Carry On

I've been working with the concept of *Stop Telling and Start Asking* since 1997 (although my parents and children will tell you I've been doing it forever). During this time, I have had the opportunity to coach a few people twice.

You're probably thinking this is because I didn't do my job right the first time.

Not so. Each of the people I've re-coached underwent a major job change, either within the same company or by moving to a different corporate culture.

One in particular stands out.

. . .

One of the Big Four accounting firms hired me to coach Neil on his path to becoming a partner. I will never forget our first meeting. Neil was—and remains—one of the nicest people I have ever met. Born, raised, and educated in the Midwest, he has a wife he adores, a young family, a promising career, an affable disposition.

The first question I ask is, "Why do you want to be a partner here?"

"Wow, no one has ever asked me that before."

He thinks for a while and then says, "I have a master's in taxation and fourteen years of tax work under my belt. What else would I do?"

"Do you really think this is the only thing you can do?"

"I honestly have never thought about doing anything else—except for the time I applied to be CFO for the Denver Broncos."

He shows me the framed rejection letter that he has hanging in his office. We laugh.

"It's my job to help you figure out what you want and how to get you there. I'd like you to think about other possible opportunities, but we will move forward assuming you want to be partner here."

And that's what we do.

Neil has a few habits to break. He is truly a funny person with a self-deprecating sense of humor. In social circles, I am quite sure Neil is very entertaining. In the professional world, however, making jokes about yourself can come off completely differently.

Neil stops making jokes about himself. It isn't easy. He has to hold his tongue more often than is comfortable. But as we focus on this, I can see Neil standing taller and projecting more self-confidence.

At the same time, we start developing his ability to ask questions.

It is an interesting transition to watch. People who know Neil are used to him making jokes about himself; suddenly they are dealing with someone more thoughtful. Neil struggles at first, especially in front of his boss or when he's with clients.

I can feel that he has moments where he squirms in his seat, wanting to joke to relieve the tension. But he stays with it. Eventually, he really "gets it" and it changes his life. He has much more control and he is much more engaged. He isn't looking for that chance to lower the pressure in the room.

At the same time, two other significant things happen. Neil gets a new client completely on his own, for the first time.

And his employer goes belly-up during a recession.

Neil ends up as a financial consultant for his recently acquired client. It's a Fortune 500 company with one of the finest nationwide sales forces in existence. The sales force operates like a group of self-employed freestanding sales teams. The home office prepares their quotas but other than that, the sales teams run their own show. The sales association, not the home office, employs Neil. It is a perfect match for Neil's skill set.

Three years into his consulting contract, Neil contacts me. He wants more coaching. I am really looking forward to this opportunity.

At our initial meeting, I realize Neil has regressed. He tells me that he's thinking about hiring an assistant because he can't keep his calendar. He is canceling too many meetings.

"I feel discombobulated," he tells me.

"What do you mean?" I ask.

"There are so many hours of preparation necessary to present to this group. They are smart, very organized, and when they ask me a question, I better have the answer. When my prep time gets short, I cancel stuff I should be doing.

It is uncomfortable all around. I am concerned about my effectiveness."

The 200 managing directors that Neil works for are Type A sales professionals. They look good, they sound good, and they each make a boatload of money. It's clear that Neil is intimidated.

But I do not think that is necessary. I know Neil better than that.

My first thought is that Neil is spending an inordinate amount of time preparing for his meetings with the managing directors. Why? Because he's the consultant, and consultants are supposed to have answers!

As we talk, he realizes that he almost never asks the sales team any questions. Instead, he waits for, prepares for, and stresses over what questions they might have for him. Neil is playing defense.

We start our work by forcing Neil to limit his prep time. At the same time, we go to work on refreshing Neil's question-asking ability. I don't know whether it is because this is the second time around, or because Neil's just a quick study, but he catches on fast.

He starts building questions into his presentation, and he starts asking, "Did I answer your question?" when he's asked to explain something. He also starts making a personal connection with people by asking about their families, their professional paths, and what they plan for retirement.

As a result, Neil begins to build relationships that transcend professional relationships. He becomes a confidant as well as a consultant. When new managing directors come on board, it becomes Neil's job to put together their executive compensation package and help them make financial choices that will work for them professionally and personally.

Here are a couple of examples of how this plays out in Neil's life.

It takes a long time in this particular industry to become a managing director. There are sacrifices that need to be made by the family, both financial and time restrictions. When the big move finally happens, most new managing directors want to buy a huge house as a Thank You for their spouse and family. But Neil has seen this move fail one too many times, especially during times of economic recession.

"I need to somehow convince them to start simple and move up as their business grows," he says during one of our meetings.

"What could you ask them?"

"Why do you need a big house?"

We laugh.

"That seems a bit direct," I say. "They'd probably feel defensive."

Neil points out that studies show that no more than 27 percent of your income should serve housing debt.

"And I have a guy who is about to buy a house that needs 42 percent of his income. I know he is doing it for his wife, but it's a really stupid financial move. It takes a few years to get the financial flow necessary to sustain that lifestyle. Even more importantly, that stress could lead to other unwise short-term decisions, and right now he needs to be thinking long-term. Buying this house would be heading down a rat hole."

"So what could you ask him?"

"I could set up the scenario I just gave you, and then ask him if he thought the house was a good idea."

"And what if he says he's been promising his wife she could have this house for the last five years?"

"I'd ask him if he thought he could explain the numbers to her. Or I'd ask him if he'd like me to talk with her. Either way, it needs to happen." He shakes his head. "Why do they do this? Why do they make these financial promises before they are really ready?"

I decide I'm not going to answer that question. "Neil, I'm wondering if you just expanded your scope."

"What do you mean?"

"Does this need to be a part of what you do as their consultant? They can get tax information from most any tax preparer, but what they need from you is sound, yet compelling, advice, and they need it early in the process. I think you can really make a difference here. What do you think?"

"I think it borders on being nosy."

"Put the shoe on the other foot. How would you feel if you wanted to buy your wife a house that was not within your financial means, and your financial consultant suggested, with very good reason, you wait five more years until your business volume can better sustain the cost?"

"I'd be thankful, but stressed out at the same time."

"What if your financial consultant let you buy that house and three years later, you were strapped for cash like you'd never been before?"

"I see your point. If I don't ask the nosy question, I am doing my client a disservice."

"And if you just tell the client you really don't think buying that house is in his best financial interest, what would happen?"

"There's a good chance he might not hear me. I need to engage him, and the best way to do that is to ask him some questions so he comes to the decision on his own."

. . .

Another of my favorite stories about Neil: He is flying from Chicago to Los Angeles for an annual meeting and his seat happens to be next to the company's CFO. The old Neil would have pulled out a book or a few spreadsheets and hunkered down for the flight, making little or no connection with the CFO. The new Neil sits back and engages the CFO by asking her questions. He learns about her family, her professional path, and eventually he is able to talk to her about some of the challenges he is facing being the financial consultant to the sales force of her company. Not only does he learn a lot, he builds a great relationship with a key player in the company.

The story is now embedded in company folklore. The joke is that Neil asked the CFO, "Do you have any idea how much I had to pay to get the seat next to you?"

THE CHALLENGE
Recognizing When You Need a Refresher

How do you know when you need help sustaining your ability to *Stop Telling and Start Asking*?

In Neil's case, it's when he discovers he's spending too much time preparing. He doesn't trust his ability to simply ask questions in the course of having a conversation with the managing directors.

In Suzie's case, it's when she discovers that her team is not working hard enough.

In Brian's case, it is when three advertising executives walk out the door.

In Troy's case, it is when he can't communicate with his boss.

In Gus's case, it is when he tries to appease his guilt over not being able to promote Don.

There's always an underlying event that can propel you, can help you stop and say, "Why is this happening? Have I asked enough questions?"

What is frustrating you right now?

Your spouse is spending more money than you are bringing in. What would you ask her?

Your assistant is losing her hearing, causing everyone to work around her? What would you ask her?

Or maybe your last promotion, the one that turned your best friend into your direct report, is straining your relationship and you need to talk about it. What would you ask in that situation?

Write your questions down.

Remember, every challenge to solve is an opportunity to ask a question! Therefore, it's important to stay in touch with your challenges. Don't forge ahead and tell your people what you plan to do, or what you want them to do, until you've asked a few questions.

FOR FURTHER CONSIDERATION

I gave you three scenarios that might be challenging: your spouse spending more money than the household earns, your assistant losing her hearing, your best friend becoming your direct report due to your promotion.

In each of these situations, it may be necessary to have an example of what you are claiming. Be prepared. You need to be able to kindly explain the overspending, the lack of hearing and an example of your friend acting out due to your promotion. Above all remember, asking questions is about the quality of the questions, not the quantity.

- **Spouse** (We're going to assume you and your spouse have a healthy relationship.)

  I'm having a hard time with our financial situation; do you think we could talk about it?

  Last month we spent more money than we earned. I am concerned about where these habits will take us. Are you?

  What can we do differently next month?

  Do you think a written budget would help?

Is there anything I need to do differently?

- **Assistant losing her hearing**

  I've noticed you don't hear me when I speak to you from inside my office. It's not until I come out into the hallway that I get your attention. Are you okay?

  Have you noticed your hearing has been compromised?

  Have you checked to see if our health plan has services for hearing aids?

- **Best friend becoming direct report**

  Is my promotion affecting our relationship?

  Is there anything I can do to make this work better?

  Is there anything you can do to make this work better?

POSTSCRIPT

Neil does hire another employee—but it's another professional tax consultant, not an administrative assistant. He is able to grow his practice about 10 percent annually without increasing his overhead by hiring another support staff. His work/life balance is everything he wants it to be. He has become an integral part of the corporate structure; although he's still an independent consultant, he and the managing directors have an interdependent relationship that serves them both well. His future there is as bright as it could be.

Conclusion

My stories have a purpose. I share them in an effort to help illuminate the importance of asking versus telling. I have come as close as I can to finding a "process" for asking instead of telling. However, I still believe asking questions is an art rather than a science. Therefore it must be tried, molded, tested, practiced, played with and challenged.

My hope is that you will, at a minimum, try to prepare for a difficult conversation by writing down the questions you need to ask, strive to be the one who asks the hard questions, strive to identify great questions, strive to drop your agenda and check your motivation! The good news is you don't have to do all these at once. Chance favors the prepared mind, so get your questions down on paper.

When I begin a coaching assignment there is one thing I ask my clients: "Do you like me?

In general that surprises them. It is not a question we ask in the business world. Of course they say yes. I ask them this as a lead-in to the next question: "Do you think you will always like me during this process?"

Now I have their attention.

Most of them laugh. They understand where I am going. They realize that I'm going to make them work hard, that I will push them in ways that are uncomfortable.

I mention this to remind you that managing by asking questions is not supposed to be easy. You will be uncomfortable when you first start doing this.

Don't give up. Try it out in all areas of your life: when your flight is delayed and you need to reroute, when the dry cleaner shrinks your best suit, when you son or daughter wants to go to Mardi Gras at seventeen, or when your spouse wants to buy a house you don't think your family can afford. Ask questions.

A few weeks ago one of our college-age sons was home. One of his high school buddies was having relationship challenges and he came to our house to talk with our son. I was working in the next room. I usually don't listen in on other conversations when I am focused on working, but I couldn't help hear my son ask his friend, "What is it you want out of this relationship that you are not getting?"

Not bad for a twenty-year-old.

Asking questions works. You will develop the people around you if you start asking questions. You will develop the people around you if you continue to ask questions. It is my firm belief that this is a way of life. I hope you choose it.

If I can help, send me an email. Here's how you can get hold of me:

Maureen@cr8iveenergies.com

And be prepared. I will ask you a *lot* of questions.

Acknowledgments and Thanks

Writing a book sounds much sexier than it is. Thankfully, I had a great team behind me to push me along. I'm grateful to

My sons, Daniel, Michael and David—every Rosh Hashannah you said, "Get your book written!" and you put up with a mom who asked way too many questions. You are my true purpose here on earth.

My steps, Lauren, Ryan and Erin—you stayed interested and believed I could do this.

My sisters, Kathleen and Colleen, and my brother, Drew—when I told Drew I wanted to write a book, he went out and bought me a beautiful pen, because you work better when you have the right tools.

My dad—he coined the phrase "Maureen! Stop! Breathe! Now make a declarative statement!"

My mom—to this day she still shares the love of reading with me.

My writing group at Redbird Studios, especially Judy Bridges—you are the best of the best.

My editor, Anne Bingham—what patience!

My book designer, Sue Knopf—such talent!

My cover designers, Doug Fellows and Kate Hawley—you rock.

My publication consultant, Susan Pittelman—you brought it all together.

My readers, June Kriviskey, Laurie Segal, Ruth Graczkowski, Dan Kadlec, Kim Kadlec, Joanie Kelsey, George Stanley, Drew Blanchfield, Mike Beno, and Pam Kasper—thank you for your time, willingness and responses.

Diana Waterman, Ellen Powers, Mark King and Julie Peck, four amazing role models who taught me so much—I am who I am in part because of you.

My clients—you let me into your lives and let me learn from you. There is a piece of each of you in this book.

Nikki—your fight for life inspires me every day.

And Keith—you believed in me before I believed in myself—your love carries me.

About the Author

Executive coach and professional speaker Maureen Kolb is dedicated to serving others by helping them see things from a different perspective. Born in New Jersey, Maureen also lived in New York and Wisconsin before attending college at the University of Wisconsin-Madison where she majored in Political Science and Women's Studies. Her early career was spent as a legislative aide on Capitol Hill, which she says was a great place to learn the importance of asking questions.

Maureen spent ten years in sales, working in Milwaukee, Wisconsin. This experience provided yet another opportunity for her to learn the value of asking questions. It was Maureen's work as a certified ropes course instructor, however, that was the catalyst for her understanding the need to develop people at all levels. In this role she met business teams that clearly would have benefited from learning to simply *Stop Telling and Start Asking*.

Prompted by her belief that people need to mentally walk in each other's shoes in order to fully understand one another, Maureen founded Cr8ive Energies in 2004. Her consulting practice at Cr8ive Energies includes executive coaching, large group facilitation, and public speaking. The primary focus of her practice is based on her conviction that in order to grow the people around us, we have to *Stop Telling and Start Asking*.

Maureen and her husband Keith live in Fox Point, Wisconsin. They have six grown children. In her free time Maureen enjoys mountain climbing, touring foreign countries by bicycle, playing golf, and reading.